D1171569

The Book
of Warsaw
Palaces

Tadeusz S. Jaroszewski

The Book of Warsaw Palaces

Photographs by Edmund Kupiecki

Interpress Publishers 1985

ISBN 83-223-2048-5

This book, which we have the pleasure of presenting to the public, comprises concise information on fifty palaces and residences in Warsaw and its neighbourhood. Naturally, this does not include all palaces and residences which existed in Warsaw and its vicinity, only those which have preserved their artistic merits and were rebuilt from wartime destruction back to their original aspect. On the other hand, the Royal Castle, the Łazienki Palace, and the Palace of Wilanów are not described here for the simple reason that many books have already been published on each of those splendid residences. Alongside of 17th and 18th century mansions, much attention has also been given to 19th century residences and villas which, until recently, were considered of small interest and consequently omitted from books of this kind.

Incidentally not many books on Warsaw deal with the subject which interests us here. Aleksander Kraushar's *Dawne pałace Warszawskie* (Warsaw's Old Palaces), published in 1925, contains descriptions of only four of Warsaw's residences. The little book by J.P. Zajączkowski, published in 1976, discusses thirty-eight residences, but the work is already out of date. The intention of Tadeusz Jaroszewski, the author of this book, was to provide as full and comprehensive a review of Warsaw's palatial architecture

The Brühl Palace in 1918–39

The Jabłonowski Mansion (town hall) in 1918–39

as possible. He also hoped to give new life to old anecdotes and historical facts, thereby bringing the noble structures he describes, and their former occupants, closer to the reader. Writing the history of those residences, Jaroszewski used information obtained through his own research, and that by other historians of art. He also made use of little volumes on various architectural monuments which form part of that excellent series entitled Warsaw's Historic Buildings published by the State Scientific Publishers, and papers by graduates of the History of Art Institute, Warsaw University, particularly those dealing with Warsaw's 19th century palatial architecture.

The photographs in this book are by Edmund Kupiecki, who specializes in period architecture. They show the beauty of Warsaw's mansions which were painstakingly rebuilt after the Second World War. In order to give readers a complete picture of Warsaw's palatial architecture, and understanding of the vastness of wartime losses, illustrations also include photographs of the Brühl, Jabłonowski, Kronenberg and Rzyszczewski mansions, and the Saxon Palace, which have not been rebuilt.

5 This volume, though not a guide to Warsaw's historic buildings, is

intended to encourage the reader to visit the noble residences of the capital, without suggesting any specific itinerary. Descriptions of individual palaces and residences are given in alphabetical order, according to names of their former owners or names by which they have been traditionally known. Most of these residences lie along the historic route which leads from the Royal Castle to the Belvedere Palace, and also along Miodowa Street, as well as Długa and Senatorska Streets which branch off it. No palatial residences were built within the old city walls, for the good reason that there was no space available for such great edifices; they were built in what were then suburbs of Old Warsaw. The principal feature of Warsaw's 17th and 18th century residences was a large court-of-honour in front of the entrance to the building which had wings at right angles to it on either side. Residences built along the street came relatively late, toward the end of the 18th century, and were popular throughout the 19th. Palatial villas, which became fashionable in the reign of Stanislaus Augustus, last king of Poland, were usually built along the old western embankment of the Vistula, and in the 19th century, along Ujazdowskie Avenue and Foksal Street. Most Warsaw residences were built in neo-classical style or in different versions of the

The Kronenberg Residence in 1918–39

The Rzyszczewski Residence in 1918–39

renaissance style, extremely popular with 19th century architects.

It should be remembered that only a few of Warsaw's residences escaped destruction in the last war, namely the Belvedere Palace, the Dziewulski, Janasz, Karnicki, Sobański and Wierzbicki residences, the residence of Eliza Wielopolska, the Council of Ministers Palace (former Radziwiłł residence), the mansions at Natolin and Ursynów. All other residences were destroyed by the Nazis in 1939 or 1944. After the war, through the efforts of the new authorities, they have been painstakingly rebuilt.

Belvedere Palace UL. BELWEDERSKA 1

The Belvedere Palace stands in picturesque grounds in an English style park on the edge of the Vistula embankment, which links up with the Łazienki Park. The charm of the spot was first noticed in the 17th century by Krzysztof Pac, Lord High Chancellor of the Grand Duchy of Lithuania, who in 1659 decided to have a small suburban residence built there for his wife; the house was completed in 1663. Because of the beauty of the view, the property was given the name Belvedere, which means beautiful vista in Italian. It is not known what the residence looked like in those days; all that is known is that Klara Izabella, née de Mailly Lascaris, wife of Krzysztof Pac, left the property to their adopted son Kazimierz Michał Pac, Record Keeper of the Grand Duchy of Lithuania. In her will, the Belvedere was referred to as a palace, and the grounds in which it stood were called Italian Gardens. In the first half of the 18th century, the Belvedere Palace changed hands repeatedly, eventually going back to the Pac family. About 1740, on the site of the former building this family had a late baroque two-storey residence with a mansard roof built according to a design by Józef Fontana. In 1767, the property was acquired by King Stanislaus Augustus who opened the Royal Manufacture of Belvedere Porcelain in an annex of the residence. He also intended to build a great palace there which was to close the view down Ujazdowskie Avenue, but this plan had to be abandoned owing to the financial difficulties which were always troubling Stanislaus Augustus. All that remains of this project today, are plans and drawings executed between 1776 and 1779 by the well-known architect Jan Chrystian Kamsetzer.

After the king's death, the property passed to his nephew, Prince Joseph Poniatowski, and then to the Kicki family, who sold it in 1818 to the government of the Kingdom of Poland (formed from part of the Russian partition zone by the Congress of Vienna, with the tsar as king). It served as the residence of the Supreme Commander of Polish Armies, Grand Duke Constantine, brother of the Tsar Alexander I. The grand duke ordered a new residence to be built there, according to plans by Jakub Kubicki. Work was completed at the end of 1822. Kubicki converted the late baroque residence into a neo-classical country house. To give the building the distinguished character demanded of a residence of a grand duke, the architect ingeniously combined the two-storey main body of the building with two one-storey wings at right angles, which formed an imposing court-of-honour. About the year 1822, three decorative structures were built in the palace grounds: an Egyptian Temple, an Orangery in neo-gothic style and a neo-classical Temple of Diana. The grand duke and his wife Joanna Grudzińska (who was created Duchess of Łowicz), resided in the Belvedere Palace till the outbreak of the November Insurrection in 1830. It may be interesting to note that Chopin gave several concerts for the grand duke in the Belvedere. Incredible as it may sound, the park and grounds were kept in order by citizens condemned to compulsory labour for petty offences and chained to wheelbarrows. This penalty was imposed on workmen, craftsmen, tradesmen and shopkeepers, students and even schoolboys. In the

19th century the Belvedere Palace was the property of the Russian tsars. During the First World War, it served as the residence of the German Governor-General Hans Hartwig von Beseler. After the First World War, the Belvedere Palace was taken over by the Polish government, as one of the state residences. Marshal Józef Piłsudski, then Head of State, was first to reside there; in 1922 the Belvedere became the official residence of the President of the Republic. After the assassination of President Gabriel Narutowicz, the Belvedere was used by President Stanisław Wojciechowski. Following the coup d'état of May 1926, Marshal Piłsudski returned to the Belvedere Palace where he resided until his death in 1935.

During the last war, the Germans did important conversion work to the building (which continued from 1940 till 1943), to turn it into a residence of Governor-General Hans Frank. In 1945, the Belvedere Palace became the residence of the President of the Polish Republic, and now serves as residence of the Chairman of the Council of State. The Belvedere Palace is one of the few residences in Warsaw which escaped destruction during the war.

Front view of the main building   View from the garden

View from the street

The Pompeian Room

Palace of the Bishops of Cracow UL. MIODOWA 5

At the end of the 16th century, the site where the Palace of the Bishops of Cracow now stands was occupied by a wooden house of a Warsaw tailor, and next to it a malt-house. In 1597, the whole site was acquired by George Frederick, Margrave of Brandenburg and Duke of Prussia, who intended to build a residence there which would serve him during his visits to the Polish capital. His successor, Johann Sigismund, abandoned this plan and sold the property to Queen Constance, spouse of Sigismund III. The queen wanted to build a palace there, which she intended to give to the Cracow Chapter as the residence of the bishops of that diocese. Work on the palatial residence was completed by Bishop Jakub Zadzik in 1642. The palace suffered heavy damage during the Swedish Wars, and was restored by Bishop Andrzej Trzebicki in 1668. Badly damaged again in the mid-18th century, it was restored in late baroque style presumably by the architect Jakub Fontana who worked on commission for Bishop Kajetan Sołtyk between 1760 and 1762. The palace is one of the few residences in Warsaw built in line with the street. Following its restoration, the palace, or at any rate that part of it which faced Miodowa Street, was a two-storey building. The first floor, where the official reception rooms were situated, was very high. That was what it looked like on a painting by Bernardo Bellotto, called Canaletto, executed in 1775, which shows a view of Miodowa Street.

This period in the palace's history is associated with Kajetan Sołtyk (1715–88), who was Bishop of Kiev between 1756 and 1759, and Bishop of Cracow from 1759. The circumstances in which Sołtyk obtained his nomination to the Diocese of Cracow from King Augustus III were very unusual, to say the least, so much so in fact, that Bishop Ludwik Łętowski saw fit to recount them in detail in his *Memoirs*. At the time, there were two rivals for the nomination to the See of Cracow, Sołtyk and Cracow Dean Michał Wodzicki. Wodzicki had the support of the queen, while Sołtyk enjoyed the protection of the king's all-powerful minister, Henryk Brühl, and his son-in-law Jerzy August Mniszech. The Bishop of Cracow, Andrzej Stanisław Załuski, was at death's door, the whole point was which of the two rivals would get to the king first, bringing news of his death and obtain from His Majesty the nomination. "The Wodzicki family had messengers with relay horses posted all the way from Cracow to Warsaw, waiting to carry news of Załuski's death to the capital", Łętowski wrote, "while the Sołtyk family had pieces of artillery placed at regular intervals all the way to the capital. Thus the shot fired by the last gun in the vicinity of Warsaw came ahead of the rider by several hours. Sołtyk was waiting, the nomination document all prepared, needing only the king's signature. The problem was to get the king in good humour first. Sołtyk had had the king's jester bribed; at a given signal, the fellow stuffed the seat of his trousers with flock, let it catch fire at the fireplace and started running round the room, the smoke pouring out from his posterior. The king was amused and deigned to laugh heartily as the clouds of smoke poured out. On seeing this, Sołtyk put forward the nomination for His Majesty to sign, which the king did without bothering to ask what he was signing. Then Sołtyk went straight to Wodzicki where he placed a purse of gold on the table. Wodzicki took the blow like a Christian. Aware of stratagems practised in such circumstances, he had the nomination stamped and accepting the purse in token of humility, he threw the gold to his scribes. When next day the queen came to ask the king for the vacant See of Cracow on behalf of her protégé, it was too late: the matter had already been settled. It was from the queen that the king learnt on whom he had bestowed the diocese".

Kajetan Sołtyk surrounded himself with a large and brilliant retinue in the residence, which he converted to his taste. He "kept pages, dragoon guards and other officials. As his coach rounded the porch of his palace, the front rank of his guards would already be riding through the Royal Castle gates", wrote Łukasz Gołębiowski in his *Historical and Statistical Description of the City of Warsaw,* published in 1827. Later, Sołtyk disclosed himself as an opponent of reforms, hostile to King Stanislaus Augustus. Leader of the Catholic opposition in the struggle for equal rights for dissenters, Sołtyk opposed demands advanced by the Russian Ambassador Nikolai Repnin during Seym (Polish parliament) sessions in 1766 and 1767, for which he was arrested, together with three other opposition senators, and deported to Kaluga in Russia, where he stayed till 1772. On his return to Poland, he showed symptoms of mental illness. Finally, his incapacity was declared by the Cracow Chapter in 1782.

After the third partition of Poland, the palace was taken over by the Prussian government. In order to obtain some profit from the building, the ground floor was converted into shops. In the Duchy of Warsaw (1807–15), the palace housed the trade tribunal, courts of arbitration and of appeal. In 1823, the building was staked in a lottery. Half the winning ticket was bought by Natan Morgenstern of Sandomierz, the other half by three Jews from Końskowola. From them, the palace was purchased by two Warsaw burghers, Tomasz Czaban and Łukasz Piotrowski. The latter bought his partner's share in 1828 and became sole owner. He carried out a radical conversion of the building, turning it into an apartment house and dividing the high first floor into two floors. The palace underwent further conversions during the 19th century, losing all artistic merit in the process. Hit by German bombs in September 1939, it was gutted by fire. After the war, it was restored as an office building, its Miodowa Street elevation regaining its aspect from 1760–62, but the first floor was left divided into two floors. The above mentioned painting by Bernardo Bellotto proved a great help in the reconstruction. At present, the palace houses the Central Board of the Aircraft and Engine Industry.

A memorial plaque in the wall of the Senatorska Street wing commemorates a group of Polish patriots shot there by the Nazis on 15 February 1944. Another memorial plaque on the elevation facing the E-W Thoroughfare, is in honour of Wacław Gąsiorowski, popular writer of historical novels, who was born here in 1869.

View shown on the border of the plan of Warsaw drawn by Pierre Ricaud de Tirregaille, 1762

General view

Façade

The central part of the façade with a tablet commemorating the reconstruction carried out by Bishop Kajetan Sołtyk

The Blank Palace

This residence was built in all probability between 1762 and 1764, according to plans by Szymon Bogumił Zug, for Filip Nereusz Szaniawski. It was modelled on suburban Paris residences, dating from the first half of the 18th century. Like a number of residences in the Faubourg St. Germain, the main body of the building stands at the extremity of a court-of-honour surrounded by lower annexes. The entrance gate affords a view of the mansard-roofed polygonal projection surmounted by a pediment with a rococo cartouche. Its similarity to Paris residences was noted by foreign travellers visiting Warsaw in the reign of Stanislaus Augustus. Johann Bernoulli from Switzerland wrote in 1778 that "the style of the building is reminiscent of pretty little Paris palaces". Though the building was in late baroque style, in its decoration neo-classical elements are apparent alongside rococo and late baroque ornaments.

In 1776, Szaniawski sold the residence to General Aleksander Soldenhoff who in turn sold it the following year to the Warsaw banker Piotr Blank. The interiors were sumptuously appointed according to neo-classical designs by either Jan Chrystian Kamsetzer or Szymon Bogumił Zug. The vestibule with its four Doric columns and an imposing staircase, was particulary magnificent. The reception rooms arranged en suite and all facing south, occupied the first floor, and the most sumptuous of them was the oval or conch-shaped room in the central projection. Piotr Blank assembled a fine collection of paintings and sculptures.

After Blank's death, the palace changed hands several times and was converted into rented apartments. Following the collapse of the January Insurrection in 1864, it was confiscated by the Russian authorities and for two years occupied by Russian troops and a commission of investigation. The reason for the confiscation was that some of the inhabitants fought in the Insurrection.

In 1896, the building was acquired by the Warsaw Municipal Council and turned into offices. In the interwar period, it served as a residence where the Mayor of Warsaw received official visitors. Stefan Starzyński, the last Mayor of Warsaw in the interwar period, had the building restored to its original splendour. The work of restoration supervised by Stanisław Gądzikiewicz began in 1935 and ended in 1938. Following Warsaw's capitulation in September 1939, the building was taken over by the Germans and housed a German office supervising the work of the Polish city administration. It was destroyed during the Warsaw Uprising in 1944, its furnishings having been earlier sent to Germany. The palace was rebuilt by a team headed by Elżbieta Trembicka after the war. At present, the Blank Palace houses the Office of the

Warsaw City Conservator and also the laboratories and offices of the Monument Conservation Workshop State Enterprise. The memorial plaque at Senatorska Street marks the place where the poet Krzysztof Kamil Baczyński, a soldier in the Home Army, was killed on 4 August 1944.

General view

The gate and the central projection of the main building

The Błękitny (Azure) Palace UL. SENATORSKA 37

The palace got its name from the colour of the roof which covered it in the 18th century. Though this roof was taken down a hundred and sixty years ago, the name remains. The history of the residence began toward the end of the 17th century, when the ground on which it stands belonged to Teodor Potocki, chaplain to King John III, later Bishop of Warmia, and Primate of Poland. Historians believe that it was built either at the end of the 17th or the beginning of the 18th century but it is not known what it looked liked originally. In 1721 Teodor Potocki gave the residence to his brother Stefan. The mansion adjoined the grounds of the Royal Saxon Palace, and caught the eye of King Augustus II who was seeking a suitable residence for his natural daughter, the Countess Anna Orzelska. In 1726, Potocki ceded the residence to the king who gave it that same year to the countess as her personal property. Complete conversion of the residence to the style of late baroque began immediately under the supervision of Carl Friedrich Pöppelmann, Joachim Daniel Jauch and Jan Zygmunt Deybel. The former Potocki residence now became the main body of the new palace with two new wings running right up to Senatorska Street forming a court-of-honour, and a large annex was added west to the residence proper. The mansard-roof of the main building was covered with azure-blue Dresden tiles. The small garden stretching at the back featured ornamental fountains, a water-fall and an orangery. The interior was beautifully appointed with rococo gilded panelling and stucco work, paintings and objects of art.

Anna Orzelska, purported to have been one of the most beautiful women of her time, was the natural daughter of Augustus II and Henrietta Renard, daughter of a Warsaw wine merchant, born about the year 1707. Her brilliant career began when she was recognized by her half-brother Fryderyk August Rutowski (natural son of Augustus II and a Turkish girl named Fatima), who presented his half-sister to her royal father dressed in male attire. This is how Charles Louis Pollnitz, chronicler of life at the Court of Saxony, described the scene: "After inspecting a regiment of horse, the king was strolling in the palace gardens. He had just expressed contentment with the regiment's drill and general turnout, when the Count Rutowski let slip a remark that he had a young lady in his household who was as skilled in the martial arts as the best of officers. The king expressed the wish to see her and she came dressed in military uniform. The king was delighted and immediately understood from her bearing that she must be his daughter. He embraced her cordially and addressed her as Countess Orzelska. A few days later, he endowed her with a most generous pension and built her a magnificent, splendidly furnished residence. She now had her own Warsaw residence where the king and his court used to visit her regularly every evening, showing her every courtesy due to a royal daughter. Later, the king took her to Saxony where he let her see all beauties. Many ladies vied for the king's favour, but all in vain, for paternal love was stronger than any amours". Countess Orzelska's Warsaw residence long remained concrete evidence of her brilliant career. "The people of Warsaw believe that a secret underground passage exists, which connects her residence with the king's Saxon Palace", wrote the Warsaw historian Kazimierz Władysław Wójcicki.

Anna Orzelska was married to Prince Charles Louis von Holstein-Beck. On leaving Warsaw, she returned her residence to her royal father in 1730. That same year, in exchange for a life-long lease of the Wilanów Palace, Augustus II ceded the residence to Maria Zofia Denhoff, née Sieniawska, who in 1731 married Prince August Aleksander Czartoryski, later Palatine of Ruthenia. Subsequently, the palace became the residence of their son, Prince Adam Kazimierz, one of the most enlightened Polish magnates of the time and great protector of the arts, who married Izabella Flemming in 1761. In 1766–68 Princess Izabella had the ground floor converted for her personal use, according to plans by Jakub Fontana. The residence was converted again by Efraim Schroeger between 1770 and 1781, when an extra window was added at either end of the façade. This aspect of the palace was immortalized by Bernardo Bellotto. In 1811 it passed to Stanisław Zamoyski and his wife, the famous beauty Zofia Czartoryska, daughter of Adam Kazimierz and Izabella. Zamoyski commissioned Fryderyk Albert Lessel, one of the greatest Warsaw architects of the first half of the 19th century, to draw up plans of complete conversion of the palace. Between 1812 and 1819 the palace acquired its present severe neo-classical aspect. The façade bore the following inscription: YEAR OF RESTORATION OF THE KINGDOM, in commemoration of the fact that work was completed the year in which the Congress of Vienna constituted the Kingdom of Poland, viewed at the time as a partial restoration of Poland's independence. A three-storey annex designed by Józef Benedykt Schmidtner was added between 1833 and 1838 at Senatorska Street.

The palace remained in the Zamoyski family till 1945. Up to the outbreak of the Second World War, it contained a magnificent collection of works of art assembled by several generations of the Zamoyskis and in a separate house the famous Library of the Zamoyski family. The latter house, which connects with the right wing of the residence, was restored in renaissance style according to plans by Julian Ankiewicz between 1866 and 1868. The palace, together with priceless works of art and part of the library, was almost totally destroyed during the bombardments of Warsaw in September 1939. Work on rebuilding began in 1948 according to plans by Bruno Zborowski and Zasław Malicki. At present, it houses the Warsaw Municipal Transport Offices.

A view of the Azure Palace by Zygmunt Vogel. 1785

Front elevation

Garden elevation of
the main building

The Library

The Borch Palace (also known as the Archbishops' Palace) UL. MIODOWA 17/19

In the third quarter of the 17th century, a wooden manor-house belonging to Aleksander Połubiński, Marshal of the Grand Duchy of Lithuania, stood on this site. In 1681, the manor-house became the property of Wawrzyniec Wodzicki and in the 18th century it was purchased by a well-known banker, Baron Piotr de Riacour, who built a baroque residence there. In 1768, the baron's son, Andrzej de Riacour, a diplomat in the service of Saxony, sold the palace to Jan Borch, Deputy Chancellor, later Palatine of Livonia and finally Lord Chancellor of the Crown. Presumably in the 1780s, the palace was converted to neo-classical style according to plans by Dominik Merlini. In 1800, when Warsaw was part of the Prussian partition zone, Michał Borch sold the building to Ludwik Nesti, a confectioner who opened a popular café and restaurant there. Between 1810 and 1837 the building was owned by the Kerner family. In his work on the history of Miodowa Street, Franciszek Maksymilian Sobieszczański wrote: "This building is also a memento of a generous reward for courage and fidelity. In his youth, Prince Joseph Poniatowski served in the Austrian army, where he came to know a Croatian soldier Karol Kerner; in one of the skirmishes with the enemy, the prince, carried away by his boundless courage, found himself in peril and was saved thanks to Kerner's presence of mind; when the prince left Austrian service he took Kerner to Warsaw, kept him among his retinue, rewarded him generously, and in 1810 bought the old Borch residence for him from Ludwik Nesti." Before the year 1830, the building housed a hotel and restaurant named Hotel d'Europe, run by Simon Chovot.

The government of the Kingdom of Poland acquired the building in 1837. For a time, it housed the Alexander Finishing School for Young Ladies, later transferred to Puławy. In 1843 the former Borch palace became the residence of the Metropolitan Archbishop of Warsaw and was completely restored. Burnt down during the Warsaw Uprising in 1944, it was rebuilt after the war and now serves as the residence of the Primate of Poland. An attractive rococo summer-house built in the mid-18th century, stands in the gardens at the back of the palace.

Gate leading to the courtyard

The main building

Central projection of the main building

View from the garden

The Branicki Palace

UL. PODWALE 3/5, UL. MIODOWA 8

The Branicki Palace, one of Warsaw's finest late baroque residences, owes its existence to Jan Klemens Branicki, Castellan of Cracow, Grand Hetman of the Crown. Work on the palace began about the year 1740, certainly not before. Three years later a serious misunderstanding occurred between Branicki and his architect, Jan Zygmunt Deybel. Branicki dismissed Deybel and in his place engaged Jan Henryk Klemm, a well known Warsaw builder, to do the finishing work and supervise interior decorations. The palace consisted of the main building (its back elevation facing Miodowa Street), and two wings at right angles which formed a court-of-honour opening on Podwale Street. The front of the central building has a four-columned portico surmounted by a group of allegorical figures supporting a cartouche with the Branicki armorial bearings.

Klemm's follower as Branicki's architect was Jakub Fontana who supervised construction of service annexes between 1750–54, designed a late baroque pavilion attached to the wing of the palace off Senatorska Street, built in 1753–54, and was in charge of redecoration of the interior in 1757.

After the grand hetman's death, his third wife Izabella, née Poniatowska, sister of King Stanislaus Augustus, continued to reside in the palace up to the year 1804, when she sold it to Józef Niemojewski and his wife Julianna, née Klug. The Niemojewskis engaged Fryderyk Albert Lessel to alter the left wing of the palace. Lessel also designed two three-storey annexes in neo-classical style on either side of the main entrance gate in Podwale Street, which had been completed by 1805. The Niemojewskis divided the residence into three parts, two of which they sold in December 1805 to Józef Pisarzewski and a certain Schneide, and the third, namely the main body, to Stanisław Sołtyk, former Lord High Steward of the Crown, in 1808. In 1817 the palace proper was sold to the merchant Józef Dyzmański, who converted the ground floor of the main building facing Miodowa Street into shops, one of which was the famous book-shop and printing house of Gustaw Leon Glücksberg, which existed there between 1839 and 1863. Until 1870, the Miodowa Street façade had a roofing resting on pillars.

The palace changed owners repeatedly in the 19th century, underwent a number of conversions, was turned into a rented apartment house and gradually lost all ornaments and artistic merit. It was hit by German bombs in September 1939 and burnt down. Rebuilt according to plans by Borys Zinserling between 1949 and 1953, it was destined for the Ministry of Higher Education. Zinserling's purpose was to restore the residence to the appearance it had when painted by Bernardo Bellotto. Thus, he decorated the palace parapet with sculptures which figure in Bellotto's painting though in actual fact had never adorned the residence. These statues were executed by a group of leading artists from the Workshop for Conservation of Monumental Architecture. The two annexes facing Podwale Street were rebuilt in the original style which Albert Lessel had given them. The palace was occupied by the Ministry of Higher Education between 1953 and 1966, and by the Science and Technology Committee between 1966 and 1972. Since 1972, it has housed the Ministry of Higher Education, Science and Technology.

View shown on the border of the plan of Warsaw drawn by Pierre Ricaud de Tirregaille, 1762

Gate leading to the courtyard from Podwale Street

Façade from Miodowa Street

The Branicki Residence

UL. NOWY ŚWIAT 18/20

At the end of the 18th century, the residence of the Badeni family stood on this spot. It is not known when it was built or what it looked like. In 1819, the property belonged to Konstancja Bilicka and comprised the main building situated at the back of the site, two annexes in the front, an outbuilding, wooden stables and a coach-house at the back. In 1852, it belonged to Wincentyna Lewińska and later passed to the Branicki family, when it was completely rebuilt as it is today in renaissance style, according to Henryk Marconi's design. The three-storey main building is in the shape of a reversed letter L. The residence faces Nowy Świat Street and is enclosed on both sides by two-storey former annexes. The left annex adjoins another two-storey house, its façade harmonizing perfectly with the architecture of the palace. The right annex, on the corner of Smolna Street, has been occupied by a chemist's shop since 1851. The entire shop fittings and décor are in gothic style; in fact, this is one of the most attractive chemist's shops in the country, in which an authentic 19th century atmosphere still prevails.

On 1 January 1899, the residence passed to Ksawery Branicki, owner of the Wilanów Palace, who had several large apartment houses built along Smolna Street. Ksawery Branicki, one of the richest men in the Kingdom of Poland, president of the Hunting Club, was famous for his avarice. Jan Kruszewski mentions in his book *Przed pół wiekiem w stolicy* (The Capital Half a Century Ago), that when Branicki arrived at the Club for dinner, "the maître d'hôtel always offered him a menu specially prepared for his lordship. This menu, alongside other dishes, also included one made specially for Branicki, priced at ten kopecks, which was usually smoked sausages served hot with horseradish sauce. If by misadventure the maître d'hôtel had forgotten to prepare the special menu, his lordship would scrutinise the list of dishes with distaste, remark peevishly that there was nothing fit to eat, and order a cup of tea and sandwich. He never tipped the club porter more than three kopecks for helping him on with his coat. If he had no smaller change than a five kopeck-piece, he would place the coin on the counter, and calmly wait for two kopecks change".

In the interwar period, the residence housed the British Embassy. The main building was destroyed during the war. Rebuilt, it now houses the Registrar's Office for Warsaw-Centre District.

Portico of the main building

General view

Portico of the main building

Gate leading to the courtyard from Smolna Street

The Brzozowski Residence

UL. BRACKA 20

Little is known about this residence. It stands at the back of an apartment house in neo-renaissance style which was built in 1848 according to designs by Henryk Marconi. The residence was built much later, in 1882 in fact, in baroque style, according to designs by Bronisław Żochowski-Brodzic. The courtyard at the back of the apartment house was divided in two by an iron railing with two gates and an attractive porter's lodge. Until 1945, the residence and the apartment house were the property of the Brzozowski family. Both burnt down during the Warsaw Uprising in 1944. When the apartment house was rebuilt after the war, another storey was added to it. The residence was also rebuilt and at present houses the Central and Regional Boards of the Polish Lawyers' Association, and also the editorial offices of the periodical *Prawo i Życie*. The palace is now one of the busiest spots of the city centre. The ground floor of the apartment house, both front and back, is occupied by various small shops. The heavy pedestrian traffic, the brilliantly lit display windows and neon lights contrast with the elegant façade of the residence which stands concealed at the back of the courtyard behind the apartment house. The residence has been immortalized in Polish literature. In the first volume of his novel, *Sława i Chwała* (Fame and Glory), Jarosław Iwaszkiewicz described it as follows: "The little palace in Bracka Street was practically surrounded by a great apartment house of many storeys, which discreetly shielded the noble residence and at the same time brought a very welcome revenue from rents, despite the recently introduced law on protection of lodgers; above all, it was a peaceful haven for the old princess, whose fortune had practically vanished, for her daughter-in-law still suffering from shock after her Ukrainian experiences, and her fine grandson Alec... The reception rooms of the Bracka Street residence were situated on the ground floor, the suites of both ladies and Alec were on the first floor. A long corridor with small bedrooms on either side, cut across the second floor, leading to the kitchen and servants staircase." Hidden away behind the apartment house, the residence remains practically unknown. It has escaped the notice of art historians, which is a pity, because its elegant neo-baroque architecture is very much worth noticing.

General view

Fragment of the front elevation

The Czapski Palace

In the first half of the 17th century, a wooden manor-house belonging to Aleksander Ludwik Radziwiłł stood on this site. After his death in 1654, the property passed to his son Michał Kazimierz, Deputy Chancellor and Field Hetman of the Grand Duchy of Lithuania. Before his death in 1680, Michał Kazimierz Radziwiłł began to build a residence there, but only the foundations had been laid when work was interrupted by his death. In 1681, the site was acquired by Michał Radziejowski, Bishop of Warmia, who became cardinal in 1686, and Archbishop of Gniezno in 1687. The residence was completed before 1705 presumably according to designs by the famous Dutch architect Tylman van Gameren, who also built Radziejowski's mansion at Nieborów. The cardinal's heir, Michał Prażmowski, sold the residence in 1712 to Adam Sieniawski, Grand Hetman of the Crown, who had it converted between 1717 and 1721. Three architects were in charge of the work, Augustyn Locci, who built the Wilanów Palace for King John III, Karol Bay, who designed the Church and Monastery of the Nuns of the Visitation in Warsaw, and Kacper Bażanka, one of the best Polish 18th century architects, to whom plans for conversion of the residence are attributed. The conversion gave the residence its present appearance, with central projections on the front and garden elevation, and corner pavilions. When Adam Sieniawski died in 1726, the residence passed to his daughter Maria Zofia, who later married Prince August Aleksander Czartoryski, subsequently Palatine of Ruthenia. In 1732, the Czartoryskis sold the residence to the banker Piotr de Riacour. The agreed price for the property was 170,000 zloties, but Riacour paid out only 10,000 in cash, the rest was written off the debt Maria Zofia had incurred with the banker. Maria Zofia, who adored beautiful clothes, was famed for her unbounded extravagance, and so it was not surprising that the story should go round that "she had traded her residence to Riacour in return for fine lace".
In 1736, Riacour sold the property to the Czapski family, who in 1743 and 1744 engaged the Italian sculptors Antonio Capar and Samuele Contessa to embellish the palace.
Further work on the residence was conducted between 1752 and 1765 when the building was converted to late baroque style, which it retains to this day. When Tomasz Czapski died in 1784, the residence passed to his daughter Konstancja married to Dominik Radziwiłł, and after his death to Stanisław Małachowski. About the year 1790, Jan Chrystian Kamsetzer designed two annexes in neo-classical style, both containing apartments to let. It is believed that Kamsetzer also rearranged some of the palace interiors.
When Stanisław Małachowski died in 1808, the residence passed tho his stepdaughter, Maria Urszula Radziwiłł, who was married to Wincenty Krasiński. Their son was the great national poet Zygmunt Krasiński. In the Kingdom of Poland the residence was one of the centres of Warsaw's social and intellectual life where Wincenty Krasiński often entertained artists and writers. In 1826 the Chopin family rented an apartment in the left-hand annex

facing Krakowskie Przedmieście (their drawingroom, furnished in the style of the period, is now open to visitors). The two corner pavilions were enlarged in 1851 and 1852 by Henryk Marconi, who gave the new additions a late baroque appearance which harmonized perfectly with the rest of the building. The famous Krasiński Library was housed in the southern part of the residence.

When the poet Zygmunt Krasiński died in 1859, the residence passed to his son Władysław, deceased in 1873, and then to his grandson Adam. In 1909, Count Edward Raczyński inherited the residence, which remained his property till 1945. Appointed Ambassador to the Court of St. James in the period between the wars, Raczyński leased the residence to Foreign Minister Józef Beck.

Between 1865 and 1867 a new street was laid along the side of the residence, then named Berg Street (now Traugutta Street). In 1867, a storey was added to the main body, making it level with the corner pavilions. About the year 1890, the two annexes were restored and altered according to designs by Julian Ankiewicz, and in 1893 Jan Heurich the Elder and Stefan Szyller redecorated some of the apartments.

In September 1939, the residence was bombed and burnt down and the annexes met with the same fate during the Warsaw Uprising in 1944. In 1946 the ruins of the residence were handed over to the Academy of Fine Arts and in 1948 Stanisław Brukalski and his team set about restoring the exterior to what it had been in the middle of the 18th century. Work continued up to 1959. The interior did not regain its original appearance. The building houses the Rectorate of the Academy of Fine Arts, its Library and some of the studios. Other studios occupy the annexes which were completely converted. A copy of the famous Venetian equestrian statue of Colleoni, Szczecin's gift to Warsaw, stands in front of the main building just off Traugutta Street.

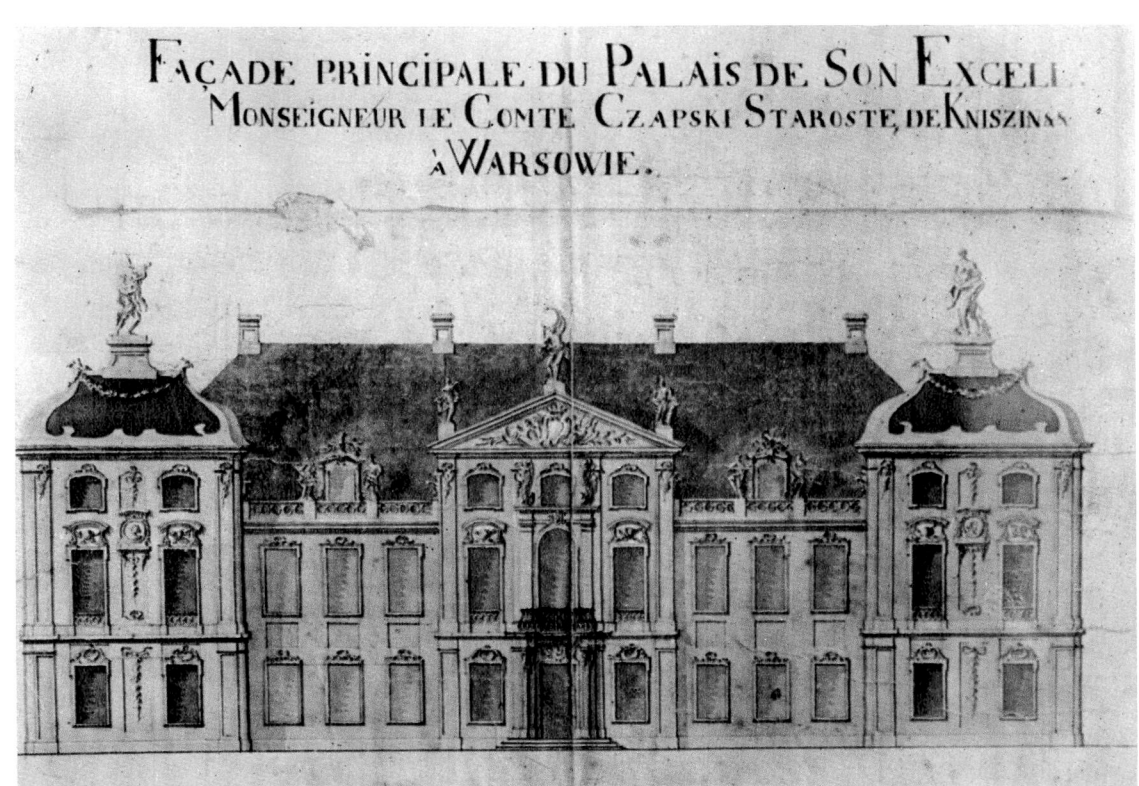

Front elevation in c. 1750

Front elevation

Portal facing Traugutta Street

The Dziewulski Residence
AL. UJAZDOWSKIE 33/35

The property on which this villa stands was purchased in 1909 by the well-known lawyer and economist, Stefan Dziewulski, and his wife Antonina Maria, née Natanson. Being in fact the last really luxurious residence built in Ujazdowskie Avenue, it was designed by Henryk Marconi in late renaissance style. Its picturesque irregular shape harmonizes perfectly with the earlier residences along Ujazdowskie Avenue. The central feature of the interior is a large hall and an imposing staircase. When Stefan Dziewulski died in 1941, the property passed to his widow and five children. The residence was one of the lucky ones which escaped damage during the last war. In 1946, Dziewulski's heirs sold it to the Bulgarian government and since then it has served as the Bulgarian Embassy.

Front elevation

The Gniński Residence (Ostrogski Castle)

The name Ostrogski Castle, now erroneously given to this residence, is linked with the person of Prince Janusz Ostrogski, Castellan of Cracow, who was the owner of this piece of land at the close of the 16th century. After his death in 1620 the property passed to the Princes Zasławski, and then to the Denhoff family. About the year 1681, it was acquired by Jan Gniński, Deputy Chancellor of the Crown, who commissioned Tylman van Gameren to draw up plans of a mansion. The architect designed an imposing residence consisting of the palace proper, which was to stand on terraced land jutting out toward the Vistula, and two detached annexes on either side of the main building. This plan however remained on paper only, owing to the tremendous cost of the terracing work and construction of powerful revetments. Probably still during Gniński's lifetime (he died in 1684), Tylman van Gameren reduced considerably the scale of his project. The residence was to consist of two detached buildings of which only the northern one was eventually erected on the high embankment overlooking Tamka Street. This building, in baroque style showing strong classical influence, towered high above the low buildings along the Vistula and became a characteristic landmark of Warsaw's panorama seen from the river.

In the early 18th century the residence passed to the Zamoyski family who in 1740 sold it to Walenty Czapski, Bishop of Przemyśl. In 1771 its owner was Jan Mikołaj Chodkiewicz, as testified by plans and designs preserved in the National Library in Warsaw.

At the close of the 18th century, the building served as a boarding-school for scions of noble families. At the beginning of the 19th century, the residence stood unoccupied and gradually became derelict. Its vast cellars and dungeons, allegedly stretching all the way to Książęca Street, became a refuge and hideout of waifs and strays, thieves and murderers who plied their trade by night. In his *Statistical and Historical Outline of the Development of the City of Warsaw from Ancient Times Up to the Year 1847*, Franciszek Maksymilian Sobieszczański writes of the strange figure of a man who lived in the derelict palace at the beginning of the 19th century: "Stefan Wyszotrawka, popularly called Stefanek, came to Warsaw in June 1805, from Pękałowo, the estate Lady Chodkiewicz owned in Volhynia. As long as the money he had brought with him lasted, he would buy a number of bouquets of flowers daily and distribute them to attractive buxom young wenches. Gay and amusing, he dressed with original extravagance: he usually wore a white frock-coat of old-fashioned cut, a bright-red waistcoat, black knee-length trousers, white silk or fine cotton stockings, high heeled black shoes with silver buckles and a round hat with large flaps. When his money ran out and he could buy no more flowers or food to keep himself going, he took to tailoring, altered jackets and overcoats and turned them inside out. He lived in the old ruined palace for over a year, and left Warsaw in October 1806 returning to Pękałowo, there to die shortly after aged over fifty."

In 1820, the property was purchased by Police Secretary Michał Gajewski, who restored the building and added another storey to it. He also built an annex which was to serve as a barracks. Huts which sprung up in the palace grounds were used as a market and butchers shops. During the November Insurrection, the palace served as a military hospital and later in turn a rubber-goods factory, a government "Health Centre", a hospital for those suffering from cholera, an institution for juvenile delinquents and a shelter for flood victims, until in 1854, it was bought by the Municipal Council which intended to turn it into barracks. In 1858, the palace was taken over by the Warsaw Institute of Music founded in 1821. The ceremonial opening of the new college took place on 26 January 1861. In 1914 a new concert hall was built according to plans by Stefan Szyller, adjoining the palace on the Okólnik Street side. The palace itself, repeatedly altered and converted, had lost all artistic merit. In the interwar period it housed a conservatoire and a drama school. In September 1944, it was burnt down by the Nazis. After the war, the ruins were turned over to the Frédéric Chopin Institute, (subsequently renamed Frédéric Chopin Society). Work on reconstruction of the residence, excluding the building designed by Stefan Szyller, began in 1949 and the new owners, the Frédéric Chopin Society, took it over in February 1955, during the Fifth International Frédéric Chopin Piano Competition. The chief designer Mieczysław Kuźma, having studied Tylman van Gameren's drawings preserved in the Collection of Prints of the Warsaw University Library, restored the palace to the aspect it presented at the end of the 17th century. The interior décor, on the other hand, is entirely new and employs late baroque, rococo and neo-classical motifs. At present in addition to the offices of the Frédéric Chopin Society, the palace also houses the Central Chopin Archives, a museum of keepsakes and mementoes of the great composer, a concert hall and a library.

This building is associated with one of Warsaw's most romantic legends, about a beautiful princess turned into a golden duck by a wicked witch and imprisoned in the dungeons of the residence. One version of the legend tells of a young cobbler who penetrated to the palace dungeons at midnight, in search of treasure. After wandering through endless passages he suddenly came upon a small pool, and there, swimming in the middle, was a golden duck. The duck spoke to him in a human voice, and pointed to a stone under which a hundred pieces of gold lay hidden. She told him that if he spent this money, down to the last penny, on revelry in the course of one day, he would find vast treasure and the hand in marriage of the princess who had been changed into a golden duck by a wicked wizard. The cobbler ran back to town as fast as his legs could carry him, made the rounds of every tavern and punctually at midnight next day was back in the palace dungeons. He put his hand in his pocket when suddenly a tremendous clap of thunder shook the ground, a pillar of fire and brimstone shot up from under his feet, and all vanished under the eyes of the dumbfounded cobbler. An unspent farthing forgotten deep in his pocket had prevented the golden duck changing back into a beautiful princess and sent the poor boy back to the old cobbler and his shop.

Western front

Elevation facing the Vistula

The first floor vestibule

Staircase

The Janasz Palace (also known as the Czacki Palace)

UL. ZIELNA 49

This residence was built in the years 1874–75 for the Warsaw financier Jakub Janasz, according to plans by Jan Heurich the Elder. Heurich modelled this late French renaissance building on the Parisian streetside residences. Originally the Janasz residence formed part of the line of buildings in Zielna Street. It became a detached residence only after the last war. Its characteristic feature was the high first floor, where the reception rooms were situated, which had a balcony with an artistic cast-iron railing running the whole length of the front elevation.

When Jakub Janasz died in 1893, the property passed to his widow Róża, née Goldstand, and their two daughters who sold the property to Feliks Czacki and his wife Zofia, née Ledóchowska. Feliks Czacki died in 1894; half the residence passed to his widow, the other half to their three children, Tadeusz, Stanisław and Róża. On their mother's death in 1911, by family agreement the whole residence was inherited by Stanisław Czacki and after his death in 1924, by his widow, Jadwiga, née Broel-Plater. In April 1939, the residence was bought by the Union of Polish Metallurgists. By the end of the interwar period the building had lost all characteristics of an elegant residence and became an apartment house. The war left it undamaged. After the war premises in the building were rented to various offices, which devastated the elegant interiors. During restoration the old ornamental elements of the front elevation were eliminated. Between 1970 and 1973, the building was painstakingly restored and adapted to the needs of the Central Administration of the Monument Conservation Workshops State Enterprise. The front elevation was restored as closely as possible to its original appearance, with the help of French illustrated magazines dating from the period when the residence was built and the interiors were also meticulously renovated. At present, the Janasz-Czacki mansion is Warsaw's best preserved residence dating from the second half of the 19th century.

Front elevation

Elevation facing the courtyard

First floor drawingroom

Detail of the ceiling in the drawingroom

Staircase

The Karnicki Residence

AL. UJAZDOWSKIE 39

The corner-stone of this residence was laid and consecrated on 12 June 1877. The man for whom the residence was designed by Józef Huss was Jan Karnicki, Privy Councillor, Secretary of State and Senator of the Russian Empire.

This is an attached building standing along the street. Its front elevation, designed with great attention to detail, is in high renaissance style, distinguished by elegant loggias on the first and second floors. Like many other buildings designed by Józef Huss, the front elevation shows the influence of Berlin architecture of that period, which is not surprising, in view of the fact that Huss was a student at Berlin's Bauakademie from 1864 to 1866. At the back, a three storey annex is attached to one side of the main building, jutting out into the courtyard. In 1928, a multi-storey modern apartment block was built at the back in order to increase the rentable value of the property. The residence itself was occupied by the owners only. At present, nothing is known of the original aspects presented by the interiors, though fragments of stucco ornaments are preserved to this day in some of the first floor rooms.

The property changed hands repeatedly. It survived the last war without damage and at present, after a number of conversions and alterations, it is occupied by the offices of several institutions.

Front elevation

Kazimierzowski Palace

The palace was named after King John Casimir (Kazimierz) who made it his favourite residence. According to some art historians, work on the building began in the reign of King Sigismund III, shortly before his death in 1632. Others hold that is was built on orders from King Ladislaus IV, who inherited this piece of land in 1637. Undoubtedly, the palace and grounds had been ready and complete by 1643, since they were described in Adam Jastrzębski's *Gościniec* (The Highway) published in that year. This was a royal summer residence, named in Italian fashion Villa Regia. Standing in beautiful grounds along the old Vistula embankment, it made a picturesque landmark in Warsaw's skyline. The late renaissance front elevation facing the Vistula had five great arches along the ground and first floors with a quadrangular tower at either side. The elevation facing the court-of-honour featured a picturesque staircase in the centre and on either side slim quadrangular turrets connected with the main building by ornate walling. It is believed that the Villa Regia was designed by the well-known Italian architect in the service of the Vasa Dynasty, Giovanni Battista Trevano.

During the Polish Swedish wars, the Villa Regia was looted and devastated by the Swedish army in 1656 and in 1660 it was gutted by fire. King John Casimir undertook its restoration, hence the name Kazimierzowski Palace. Restoration and enlargement of the palace was entrusted to Isidor Affaita and Titus Livius Burattini, who, in addition to being an architect, was also a physicist, mechanic, astronomer, geographer and archaeologist.

When restoration work was completed, this became the king's principal Warsaw residence, since the devastation the Royal Castle had suffered during the Swedish wars still made it unfit for habitation. After the death of Queen Marie Louise in 1667, and John Casimir's abdication, the palace remained unoccupied, and in 1678 it was acquired by John III Sobieski as his private property, but the king seldom used it. During his reign, it was occupied for a time by the French ambassador, the Marquis de Bethune, and later by the king's son, Prince Jakub Sobieski. The residence was once again gutted by fire which broke out on 28 December 1695, leaving nothing but blackened walls. Following the death of John III, the ruined palace and grounds passed to Prince Konstanty Sobieski, who ceded the property to King Augustus II in 1724 or 1725.

Between 1724 and 1733, two Saxon architects, Jan Zygmunt Deybel and Jan Joachim Daniel Jauch executed several plans for reconstruction of the palace in ornamental late baroque style. However all that was built on the king's orders was an entrance gate leading from Krakowskie Przedmieście, surmounted by a metal globe, and eight half-timbered barrack buildings situated symmetrically, four on either side of the court-of-honour.

In 1735, Augustus III ceded the whole property to the First Minister of his Saxon Cabinet, Aleksander Józef Sułkowski, on condition that the king would retain use of the barracks and stables for life. The new owner had a brickworks built in the grounds, also a stove works and a brewery; he also decided to restore the palace, which was done by Carl Friedrich Pöppelmann between 1737 and 1739 according to earlier designs by Deybel and Jauch. The new exterior of the palace showed the combined influence of Saxon late baroque and French rococo. A bulging metal dome which topped the central part of the main body was a distinct landmark in Warsaw's skyline seen from the river.

In 1765 or 1766, the palace and grounds were purchased by King Stanislaus Augustus to house his Cadet Corps, a Knights' College for scions of the nobility, which the king had undertaken to found when he ascended the throne. A fundamental restoration of the building began in 1765, according to plans by Dominik Merlini. The exteriors of the palace remained practically unchanged, the only addition being an entresol between the first and second floor, destined for cadets' dormitories.

When Warsaw was part of the Prussian partition zone, the Saxon barracks and other buildings standing in palace grounds were leased out as lodgings, mainly to craftsmen and minor clerks. The palace itself was taken over by the *Justiz-Magistrat* (Supreme Council of Justice); it also housed a pawnshop. When Napoleon's armies entered Warsaw, the building was turned into a military hospital. In 1808, the government of the Duchy of Warsaw handed over the whole property, together with all buildings, to the educational authorites. A school of law was opened there that same year, and a year later a medical college. During Napoleon's retreat from Moscow, the buildings were once again taken over to serve as a field hospital.

A violent fire which broke out on the night of 29/30 July 1814, consumed most of the buildings in the vicinity of the Kazimierzowski Palace, including the Saxon barracks. The palace also caught fire, luckily, however, the flames were quickly extinguished. Two wings running at right angles to the main body were added on the initiative of Stanisław Staszic. Designed by Jakub Kubicki in severe neo-classical style, they were completed in 1816, the whole forming one of the most imposing buildings in Warsaw with a vast court-of-honour.

The establishment of the Kingdom of Poland by the Congress of Vienna in 1815, followed by the foundation of Warsaw University by a decree of 19 November 1816, opened a new era in the history of the Kazimierzowski Palace, which, together with all adjoining buildings, was to serve as the new university. Between 1818 and 1822 two neo-classical houses, designed by Michał Kado, were built along Krakowskie Przedmieście Street, housing the Department of Fine Arts and lecture-rooms respectively. The Warsaw Lycée was transferred from the Saxon Palace to the Kazimierzowski, which also housed a library. The right wing of the palace was turned into apartments for Lycée teachers, including Mikołaj Chopin, the great composer's father, and his family, for the Rector and professors of the University. The left wing was occupied by offices of the Government Commission for Religious Denominations and Public Enlightenment.

The Kazimierzowski Palace itself, restored after the fire of 1814, was later subjected to fundamental reconstruction. The building acquired a fine neo-classical façade embellished by a portico with a bas-relief sculpture showing Apollo with Erato and Urania, attributed to Paweł Maliński. The interior was converted for the needs of the Central Library. Work on the palace continued till 1830. To this day, there is no certainty as to which architect made the plans. Two names are mentioned, Hilary Szpilowski and Wacław Ritschel, both of them lecturers at the University. About the year 1820, two neo-classical houses were built on either side of the Kazimierzowski Palace.

Following the suppression of the November Insurrection the University was closed down by the occupying authorities. For a time, the Warsaw Lycée was allowed to remain in the building. In 1840–41 Antonio Corazzi designed and built a new edifice in late neo-classical style for this school. The building was situated south of the right wing and later served the Main School, opened in 1862. About the year 1863, Antoni Sulimowski converted into renaissance style the house standing south of the Kazimierzowski Palace and connected it with a new building in the same style, facing Obożna Street. Sulimowski also converted the house north of the palace and began the conversion of the Kazimierzowski Palace itself. In 1861 he altered the two wings, replacing Kubicki's modest elevations with new façades in late neo-classical style, ornamented with pairs of pilasters in colossal order. These façades have remained unchanged to this day. It should be noted that another college also functioned there, namely the School of Fine Arts, which from 1844 occupied the former house of the Fine Arts Department.

After the collapse of the January Insurrection in 1864 both these schools were closed down. The most important building work undertaken by the Russian Imperial University was the great Library built between 1891 and 1894 in the centre of the court-of-honour by Stefan Szyller and Antoni Jasieńczyk-Jabłoński. Designed in renaissance style and showing strong classicist influence, the Library destroyed once and for all the beauty of the whole complex by blocking the view on the Kazimierzowski Palace. The library was transferred from the palace to the new building, and the palace itself once again underwent fundamental restoration. The entrance gate from Krakowskie Przedmieście, built in 1910 and existing to this day, was designed by Stefan Szyller in a mixture of late renaissance and baroque styles.

Little change was made to the group of university buildings in the twenty interwar years. The most important addition was the Auditorium Maximum, built in 1930 according to plans by Aleksander Bojemski, in modernised neo-classical style.

The university buildings suffered great damage during the 1939–45 war. The Kazimierzowski Palace and most of other buildings were either gutted by fire or destroyed with explosives. Those that remained were largely devastated by the Nazis. Restoration and reconstruction work began in the spring of 1945, when the university was reopened, and completed in 1960. The Kazimierzowski Palace was rebuilt between 1945 and 1954, according to plans by and under the supervison of Piotr Biegański. At present the arrangement of the ground and first floor resembles the appearance it presented about the year 1830; the front elevation has remained virtually unchanged, except for the balustraded parapet which was not rebuilt. The side and rear elevations were restored exactly to their appearance on paintings by Bernardo Bellotto. The arcaded terrace of the rear elevation between the two side projections was restored. The interiors, in late baroque and neo-classical style, were designed anew. At present the Kazimierzowski Palace houses the offices of the rector and prorectors of Warsaw University.

View shown on the border of the plan of Warsaw drawn by Pierre Ricaud de Tirregaille, 1762

View in c. 1840. Aquatint etching by A. F. Dietrich according to a drawing by J. F. Piwarski

Portico of the front elevation of the Kazimierzowski Palace

A bird's eye view of the university with the Kazimierzowski Palace
shown from the Vistula in the foreground

Palace of the Government Revenue and Treasury Commission

This palace came into being between 1823 and 1825, following complete conversion of a baroque residence which had belonged to the Potockis. The conversion was carried out according to designs by the well-known Italian architect Antonio Corazzi, in high neo-classical style. The palace was destined for the Ministry of Finance, which, during the Kingdom of Poland, carried the name of the Government Revenue and Treasury Commission. The main body of the building acquired a large Corinthian portico; the two wings were given small Ionic porticos facing the court-of-honour, and monumental Ionic columns facing the street. The palace was adorned with sculpted ornaments. The front portico bears a sculpture by Paweł Maliński, showing Minerva, Mercury and Jason (ancient personifications of Wisdom, Industry and Commerce), and allegorical figures representing the rivers Vistula and Bug. The frieze in bas-relief which runs along the main body and wings of the palace, adorned with garlands and putti, is attributed to Vincenti. Together with the neighbouring Palace of the Minister of Finance and the building of the Bank of Poland, both also designed by Corazzi, the palace forms an extremely harmonious whole. Corazzi's intention was to give a correspondingly imposing setting to this group of buildings. He planned to enlarge Bank Square (at present Dzierżyński Square) and lay a street from the square to Bielańska Street. This street was to open directly on the main portico of the palace. The plan was not carried out till after the last war, and the street in question was named after Corazzi.

Between 1919 and 1921, Marian Lalewicz and his team completely restored the palace which was given to the Ministry of Finance in independent Poland. Gutted by fire in September 1939 as a result of enemy bombing, the palace was rebuilt between 1950 and 1954 by Piotr Biegański and became the headquarters of the Presidium of the Warsaw People's Council. At present, it is also used by the Warsaw City Office. In the staircase of the main body, there stands a bust of the great poet Juliusz Słowacki and a memorial plaque with the following inscription: "Juliusz Słowacki Worked Here for the Government Revenue and Treasury Commission between 1829 and 1831."

The Golden Room
on the first floor
of the Kazimierzowski
Palace (overleat)

General view from Dzierżyński Square

Portico of the main building

Staircase

The Kossakowski Palace

The site on which the residence stands was purchased in 1780 from August Sułkowski by Isaac and Marianna Ollier. The Olliers' neo-classical residence had been completed by 1784. It was a two-storey building standing along the street. The façade had two side projections crowned with belvederes and a central projection surmounted by a pediment. The name of the architect who designed the building is not known. Isaac Ollier was a well-known Warsaw textile merchant, descended from a French Huguenot family settled in Berlin. His Nowy Świat house was one of the most elegant residences of the Warsaw bourgeoisie at the close of the 18th century.

In 1848 the residence was sold to the landowner, Władysław Pusłowski, who in 1849 undertook its fundamental reconstruction according to designs by Henryk Marconi. Another storey was added between the two side projections, each of which was also raised by another floor. Thus, the basic composition of the façade remained virtually unchanged in its high Italian renaissance style. In 1851, four stone figures representing Clio, Thalia, Urania and Erato, the work of Paweł Maliński, were set up along the top of the central projection which reached the height of the second floor only. At the time, the residence consisted of the main building facing Nowy Świat Street, and three annexes at the back, running at right angles to it. From a bird's-eye view, the residence resembled the letter E.

In 1858, the Kossakowski family altered the residence rooms according to designs by Francesco Maria Lanci. The ballroom and picture gallery, in the right annex were particularly imposing, both on account of their dimensions and sumptuous neo-renaissance décor. The official "house-warming party" on 4 March 1859 was a magnificent ball, reported in detail by the Warsaw press. Until the first years of this century, the palace was one of the most elegant aristocratic residences in Warsaw.

In 1905, the residence was converted into an apartment house. A large covered skating-rink, called the Palais de Glace, was built in the former court-of-honour in 1911–12, according to plans by Stefan Szyller. As the skating-rink did not prove as profitable a proposition as had been expected, it was turned into a roller-skating rink, and when that did not meet expectations either, it was closed down, the former rink being converted into a cinema, the Colosseum, which functioned throughout the interwar period. In 1930 the property was sold to the Warsaw Insurance Company.

The residence did not survive the last war. Heavily damaged in 1939, it was almost totally destroyed, including the Colosseum Cinema. The restoration of the building, almost from the very foundations, was undertaken in 1946 by the Swedish ASEA Company. Work was completed in 1949, but only the main body of the residence was rebuilt by Mieczysław Kuźma and his team. The front elevation regained its Marconi design and in 1972 the figures of the four Muses returned to their place. In 1968, the residence was taken over by the state and now houses the offices of the Company of Housing and Administrative Services for Foreign Diplomats.

Front elevation from Nowy Świat Street

Statues of Clio, Thalia, Urania and Erato

The Krasiński Palace

The Krasiński Palace is considered one of the best examples of architecture in the whole modern period in Poland. The palace was built for Jan Dobrogost Krasiński, Starost of Warsaw, from 1688 Palatine of Płock. Krasiński employed leading foreign artists working in Poland at the time; the residence was designed by Tylman van Gameren; decorations were the work of the sculptor Andreas Schlüter and the painter Michelangelo Palloni. His master builders were Giuseppe Bellotti, Giacoppo Solari, Isidor Affaita and one Maderni. Work on the building began some time after 1677 and the main structure was completed in 1682. Next to the residence there were a large two-storey annex which housed kitchens, an orangery, a fig-house and an arsenal. The whole property was surrounded by a wall. As soon as the structure was completed, work began on appointments and decoration. It took a long time, and a lot of valuable material such as marble and hard sandstone. The stone flooring, stone portals and chimney-pieces were finished in 1682. In 1682 and 1683 Andreas Schlüter completed six sculptured figures for the front and back elevations. In 1684 work on the stucco ornaments began. In 1684 and 1685, Michelangelo Palloni painted allegorical scenes on the ceiling and overdoors in the vestibule. Between 1689 and 1693 Schlüter executed bas-reliefs: the bas-relief on the front elevation shows the combat between the Roman Tribune Marcus Valerius Corvinus and a giant Gaul; the one on the garden elevation depicts a Roman general – probably the same Marcus Valerius Corvinus - driving a chariot under a triumphal arch. It may by interesting to note that the Krasińskis, who have a raven in their armorial bearings (*Corvinus*), contended that they were descended from that Roman. The front elevation was completed in 1693–94, and the garden elevation in 1695. The palace interiors were never finished, neither was a second annex built. Nonetheless, this was Warsaw's most magnificent residence at the time, overshadowing even royal palaces. It was built in late baroque style showing some influence of the classicist, characteristic of many residences designed by Tylman van Gameren.

The palace was purchased in 1765 by the state for use by the Crown Treasury Commission. The interior of the building underwent fundamental conversion between 1766 nad 1773, according to designs by Jakub Fontana. In 1782 the palace burnt down. Work of restoration supervised by Dominik Merlini was undertaken immediately and completed exactly one year later. The 19th century brought little change to the general appearance of the palace. In 1835, the open galleries on the first floor were glazed in. The annex underwent fundamental reconstruction in 1819 and 1820, according to designs by Piotr Aigner, who added another floor and gave the building a neo-classical finish. During the twenty interwar years, the palace served as the seat of the Supreme Court. Damaged in September 1939, it was gutted by fire and partly destroyed during the Warsaw Uprising in 1944. Its main body was rebuilt between 1948 and 1961 according to designs by Zygmunt Stępiński and Mieczysław Kuźma. The ruins of the annex were pulled down. At present the palace houses Special Collections of the National Library.

Front elevation

Central projection of the garden front

First floor drawing-room

The Krasiński Residence at Ursynów

Ursynów, previously known by the name of Rozkosz, is an attractive locality situated along the old Vistula embankment between Służew and Natolin. At present it is one of Warsaw's greatest new housing development. The history of this residence began on 28 April 1775, when Józef de Maisonneuve, colonel in the service of the Polish Army, lover of Princess Izabella Lubomirska, daughter of Prince August Aleksander Czartoryski, was granted a stretch of land in the vicinity of Służewiec manor-house comprising an alder-tree wood, meadow and rivulet flowing across it, by the princess's father. De Maisonneuve undertook to fence the whole property and pay an annual rent of 250 zloties for it, to the Służewiec manor, which formed part of the Wilanów estate. By 1777 the colonel had built a small manor-house for himself and other buildings on the property. In 1783, Izabella and her husband Stanisław Lubomirski confirmed Czartoryski's grant. A year later, de Maisonneuve ceded his rights to the property, including the residence he had built, to Princess Joanna Sapieha, née Sułkowska, who sold it in 1785 to Aleksandra, daughter of Izabella and Stanisław Lubomirski, and her husband Stanisław Kostka Potocki. This transaction opened a new chapter in the history of the property.

In 1785 and 1786 Stanisław Kostka Potocki, historian of art and amateur architect, had the residence in Rozkosz reconstructed. Plans were drawn up jointly by Potocki and Chrystian Piotr Aigner who also supervised the whole operation. Originally one floor was to be added to the residence, but eventually the idea was given up in favour of a neo-classical ground-floor pavilion, with a four-columned front portico. Two small annexes were built on either side of this pavilion, the right-hand one destined for the kitchens. Stables and a coach-house were also built. For a time, Rozkosz became a favourite suburban residence of Stanisław and Aleksandra Potocki.

In 1799 the property was sold to a certain Grzegorz Wykowski, who in turn sold it a few years later to Ignacy Kochanowski. In 1822 Rozkosz belonged to Julian Ursyn Niemcewicz, who toyed with the idea of changing its name to America, or Washington in commemoration of his stay in the United States. His friends dissuaded the poet from the idea, and eventually the property was named Ursynów, after the ancient cognomen of the Niemcewicz family. The poet restored the residence and outhouses, and set the park and gardens in order. After the suppression of the November Uprising, Ursynów was confiscated by the Russian authorities, and Niemcewicz left the country. The property was rented between 1832 and 1840 by the well-known Warsaw doctor Wilhelm Malcz. Later, it was acquired by Aleksander Potocki, owner of Wilanów, who gave it to his companion, Aleksandra Stokowska née Markowska.

About the year 1857, Ursynów was acquired by Eliza Krasińska née Branicka, wife of the great poet Zygmunt Krasiński, who intended to build a palatial residence there, for herself and her

husband. Plans were executed by the architect Zygmunt Rozpę-
dowski, and work on the residence continued from 1858 till 1860,
but the couple never lived there, Zygmunt Krasiński having died
in 1859 before its completion. In all probability, the old house was
incorporated in the new residence which was built on the edge of
the old Vistula embankment. This residence was a two-storey
elongated symmetrical building of rather complicated design.
Iron which was just coming into general use in building was one
of the materials used. The first floor terrace between the two side
projections of the garden elevation rested on four pairs of slim
iron pillars. Sculptured ornaments on the outside of the residence
were the work of Juliusz Faustyn Cengler. The pediment sur-
mounting the front elevation was given four allegorical child figures personifying the four seasons of the year. The sculptured figures of Fortune and Ceres were set up in niches on the two side
projections of the front elevation which is also decorated with
busts of four famous hetmans, Jan Tarnowski, Stanisław Koniecpolski, Paweł Sapieha and Stefan Czarniecki. The garden elevation features busts of four queens, Wanda, Dobrawa, Jadwiga and
Barbara. Advantage was taken of the sloping terrain at the gard-
en side of the residence to build picturesque stairs and terraces
which made the Ursynów park and gardens one of the most beautiful of its kind in the Warsaw region.
A year after Zygmunt Krasiński's death in 1859, Eliza married his
cousin Ludwik Krasiński, a brilliant energetic young man, much
younger than herself, who took upon himself the management of
her great fortune. Eliza Krasińska died in 1876, leaving Ursynów
to her second husband. When he died in 1895, the property passed
to Adam Krasiński, Zygmunt Krasiński's grandson. In 1906 Adam
Krasiński gave Ursynów to a Teachers' Training College, which
was still there during the twenty year period between the wars.
The former residence and its park suffered heavily during the
First World War. In 1915, retreating Russian troops completely
devastated the beautiful park, cutting down all the trees. The
garden stairs and terraces gradually fell into ruin. The Second
World War treated the residence and grounds kindly, and in fact
the property remained undamaged. For a time after the war, it
housed a secondary school and a horticultural school. In 1949, it
was decided that an agricultural school would be built here. The
architect Stefan Tworkowski and his assistants prepared plans of
the new buildings. The neo-renaissance residence, carefully restored, became the central feature of the new group of buildings.
Boarding-school buildings, a canteen and college aula were built
between 1950 and 1952. The aula was decorated by painters Leo-
kadia Bielska-Tworkowska and Maria Wolska-Berezowska. In
1956, the entire group of buildings was handed over to the Warsaw Agricultural University which has occupied them ever
since.

Detail of the central projection of the front elevation

Detail of the side projection of the front elevation

Detail of the side projection of the front elevation with busts of hetmans Koniecpolski and Czarniecki

The Królikarnia Residence

The name (literally: rabbit farm) of the residence and its grounds situated along the picturesque old Vistula embankment cut by wooded ravines, is derived from a rabbit farm which belonged to King Augustus II. In 1778 the site was purchased by Count Charles de Valery-Thomatis, Chamberlain to King Stanislaus Augustus, who intended to build himself a residence there. Of the several designs submitted the one by the court architect Dominik Merlini was accepted. First to be built were service annexes and a poultry-house, completed in 1779–80, followed by kitchens. The latter, which stood on the edge of the northern ravine, was a circular building modelled on the famous tomb of Caecilia Metella in Rome. Later, an underground passage was built, connecting the kitchens with the residence and with a grotto underneath the terrace at the eastern side of the house.

The residence itself was built between 1782 and 1786. It was a square-shaped villa in neo-classical style with a circular room in the centre, topped with a cupola resting on a drum. In its general appearance, it was modelled on the Rotonda near Vincenza, designed by the great Italian architect Andrea Palladio in c. 1570. The residence was surrounded with beautiful gardens. The receptions Thomatis gave there were the talk of the town. The Królikarnia became the venue of fashionable Sunday excursions by people of Warsaw since the gardens were open to the public; from 1783 an excellent *trattoria* also existed there, open to all who could afford the prices. During the Kościuszko Insurrection the Królikarnia sustained serious damage, and Thomatis himself was wounded by a Russian shell splinter. Tadeusz Kościuszko had his headquarters there from 10 to 14 July 1794.

When Thomatis died, the property passed to his children, from whom it was purchased in 1816 by Prince Michał Hieronim Radziwiłł, the last Palatine of Vilna, owner of Nieborów and Arkadia and an art collector of taste and distinction. He located some of his collections, including a gallery of paintings and part of his library, in the Królikarnia. In 1849, the Królikarnia was acquired by Ksawery Pusłowski and remained in his family up to the outbreak of the Second World War. Pusłowski was an equally distinguished art collector. He assembled a valuable library, collections of tapestry, bronzes, marble sculptures and paintings. All was lost in a fire which consumed the residence in August 1879. The mansion was faithfully rebuilt by Józef Huss with the help of plans which had been preserved and fragments of decorations which had survived the fire. Completion of the work in 1880 was commemorated by a marble plaque walled in the circular room. The residence was destroyed during military operations in September 1939. During the Warsaw Uprising in 1944 the kitchens were burnt down, the terrace and grotto under it were ruined and the park also suffered heavily. The residence was restored in 1965 according to designs by Jan Bieńkowski; the grounds were laid out by Longin Majdecki. As regards the interior, only the circular room regained its original aspect. The Królikarnia now houses the Xawery Dunikowski Museum, a branch of the National Museum in Warsaw, which was opened on 26 January 1965, the first anniversary of the death of the famous sculptor. The main part of the museum collection is made up of the gifts the artist made to the Polish Army shortly before his death, deposited later in Warsaw's National Museum. The gifts include sculptures, paintings, drawings, sketches as well as many personal items.

Front view

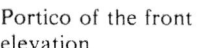

Portico of the front
elevation

Detail of the decoration of
the kitchens

The Lesser Residence

This residence was built toward the end of the 1840s for the banker Stanisław Lesser, according to plans by Franciszek Maria Lanci, who designed the building in renaissance style. Still unfinished it changed owners several times until in 1865 it became the property of Jan Władysław Kurtz. By then work on the interiors had been completed. The building was so large that Kurtz rented two apartments, leaving the third one for himself. In 1899 it was purchased by the Israel Kalmanowicz Poznański Cotton Goods Company of Łódź. During the twenty interwar years, the residence was occupied for a time by the offices of the French Embassy. In 1935, it was purchased by the coal merchant Abraham Sojka and his wife Rachel, who rented the building to the Warsaw Garrison Club. In September 1939 the residence was hit by bombs and burnt down. It was rebuilt in 1949 according to plans by Eugeniusz Wierzbicki, Jerzy Mokrzyński and Wacław Kłyszewski. The ruins of adjoining houses were pulled down, thanks to which the residence is now a detached building with a new elevation facing Matejko Street. At first the building was occupied by the Department of Party History, later by a music school and now by the Central and Regional Boards of the Union of Fighters for Freedom and Democracy. A memorial plaque on the wall facing Ujazdowskie Avenue commemorates the action by a Special Group of the People's Guard, carried out on 15 August 1943, in which hand grenades were thrown at a column of SS troops, killing and wounding thirty Germans.

The Circular Room
overleaf

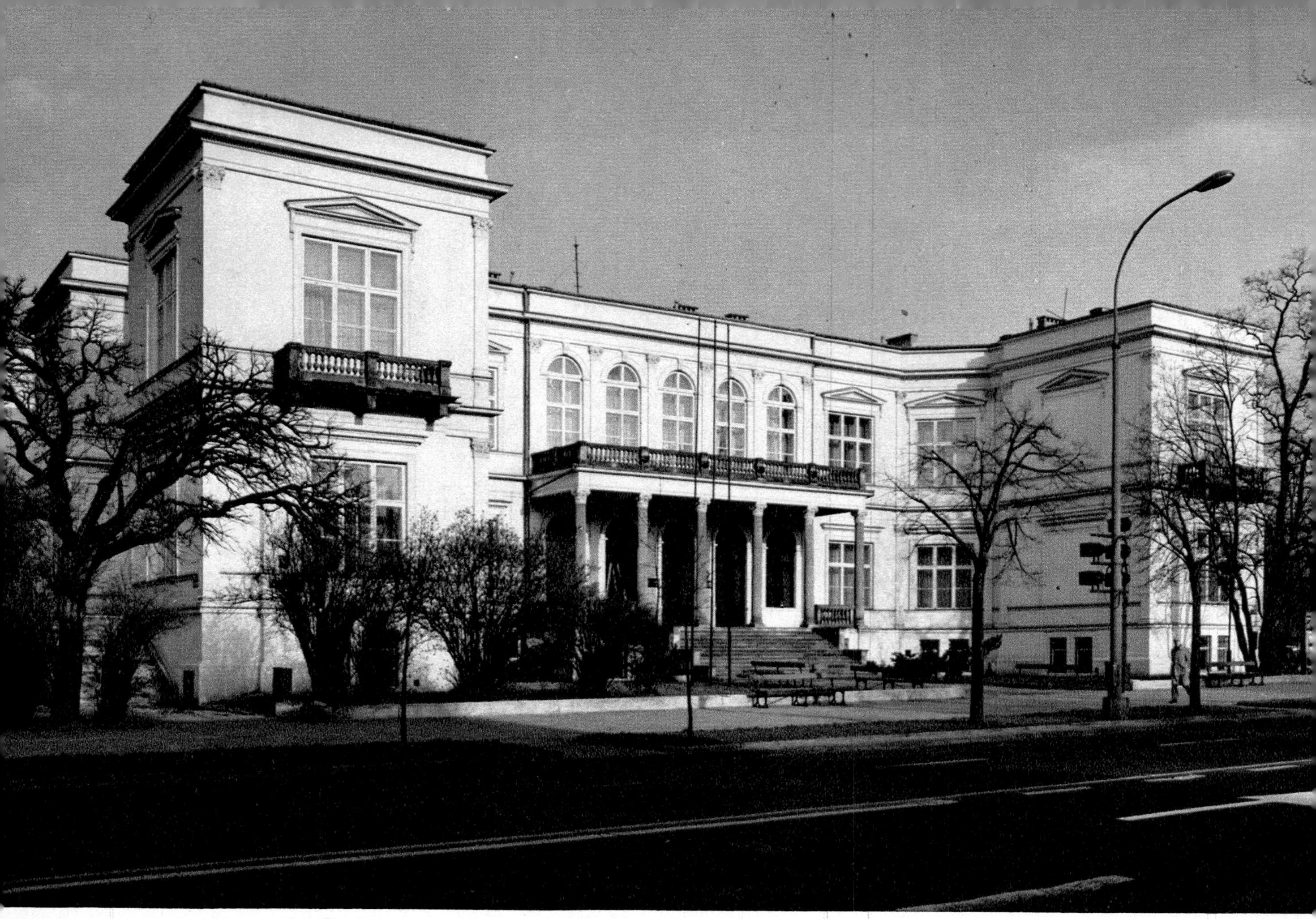

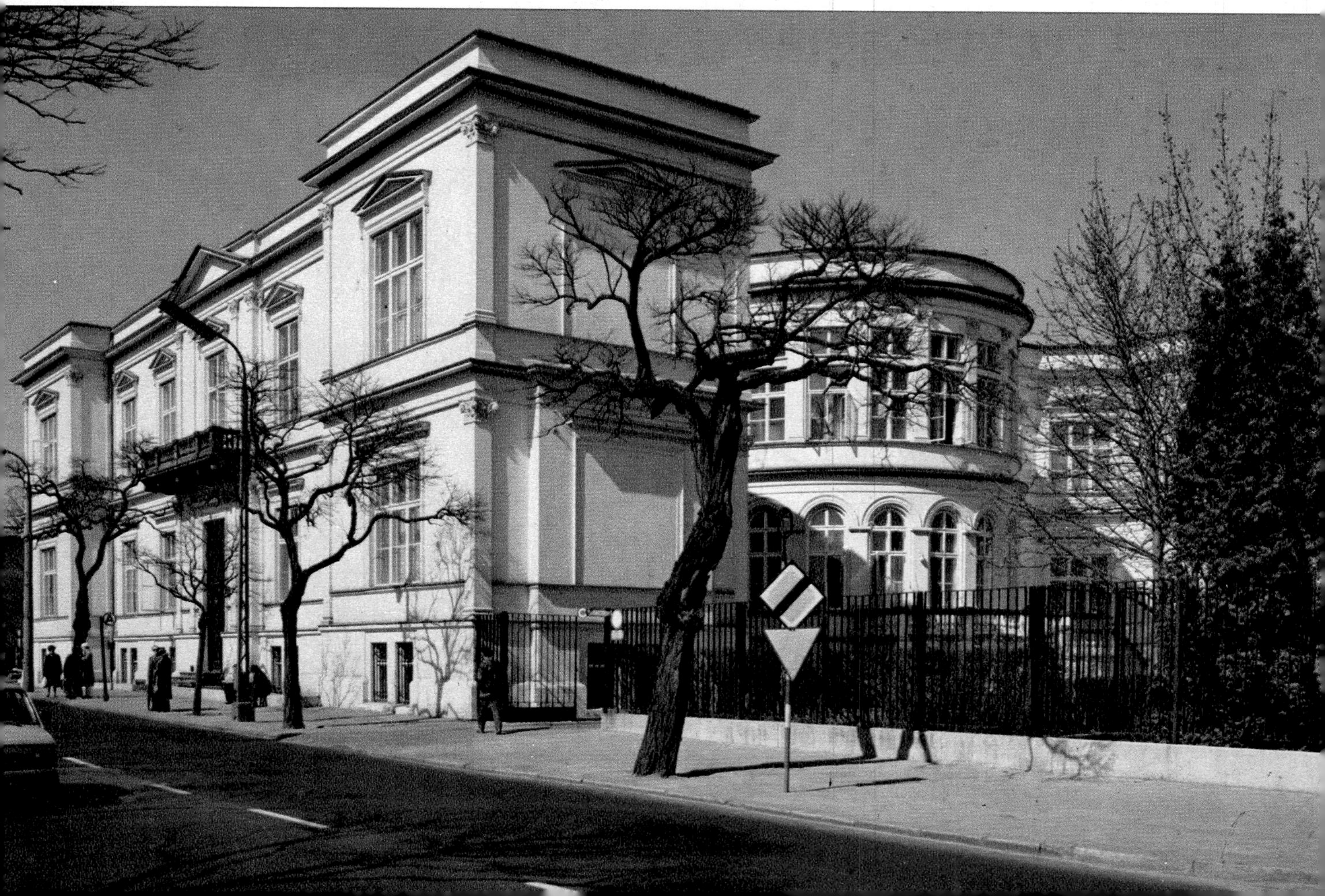

Front view

View from the south-east

Portico of the front elevation

The Lubomirski Palace

It is not known when the residence now called the Lubomirski Palace was built or who its owners were. It certainly existed in 1712, when it consisted of the main building and wings enclosing a rectangular court-of-honour. In 1730, it belonged to the architect Jan Zygmunt Deybel, and by the end of the 1730s it became the property of Prince Stanisław Wincenty Jabłonowski. About 1750 it came into the possession of Prince Antoni Lubomirski, Palatine of Lublin. In 1760 Jakub Fontana undertook fundamental conversion of the residence in the style of late baroque. The conversion was not completed, however, and this was how Bernardo Bellotto, called Canaletto, showed it in 1779. In 1776, half of the residence was taken over by Prince Antoni's ward, Aleksander Lubomirski, who inherited the whole property in 1790. The latter commissioned Jakub Hempel to prepare plans for conversion into neo-classical style. The work lasted from 1790 to 1793. The elevation facing Żelazna Brama Square, with its colossal portico of ten Ionic columns, was particularly imposing. This was the biggest colonnade in Warsaw until the Grand Theatre was built. The ground and first floors of the palace were occupied by the owner, while the second floor and wings were divided up into apartments to let. It might be interesting to note that Aleksander Lubomirski married one of the greatest beauties of the time, Rozalia, née Chodkiewicz. Rozalia was a friend of Queen Marie Antoinette; her gaiety and beauty earned her the name of la Princesse Printemps at Versailles. Rozalia shared the fate of the queen and was beheaded in Paris during the Revolution. Aleksander and Rozalia had an only daughter, also Rozalia, who inherited the residence on her father's death in 1804. Rozalia married Wacław Rzewuski, a famous traveller, who spent a large part of his life in Arabia where he was known as the Emir Tadzh-el-Faher Abd-el-Nischaane. She sold the residence to Izydor Krasiński in 1816. In 1828, the palace was purchased by the government of the Kingdom of Poland and turned into offices. During the November Insurrection it was taken over by a field hospital and following the suppression of the rising by the offices of various state institutions. The palace was sold in 1834 to the financier Abraham Simon Cohen and the gradual eclipse of the once magnificent residence began; consecutive owners kept altering and transforming the building with a thought to obtaining the greatest possible profit from it. The entire ground floor was converted to shops, and the arcaded colonnade was demolished to give room to stalls. In the 1870s the palace housed a synagogue.

In 1929, another storey was added to the main building, according to plans by Wacław Moszkowski. In 1934 the palace was sold to the Warsaw Savings Bank, from which it was purchased by the Warsaw City Council with the intention of restoring the residence back to the appearance it had been given by Jakub Hempel. The outbreak of war, however, frustrated these plans. Hit by enemy bombs in September 1939, the palace burnt down.

In 1947, the building was turned to the Museum of Archaeology, after it had been restored and adapted for museum purposes according to plans by Tadeusz Żukrowski. Later, it was taken over by the Army, which completed its restoration in 1950. Its situation at an angle in relation to Żelazna Brama Square was awkward from the point of view of urban development. Consequently, it was decided to move the whole palace so that is should conceal from view the ugly Bazaar and close the vista down the main avenue of the Saxon Gardens. Plans for the operation were prepared by Aleksander Mostowski of the Mostostal Company and the work was entrusted to the Municipal Engineering Works Company. The whole residence as it stood began moving on 30 March and reached its ultimate resting place on 18 May 1970. The palace travelled to its new position on sixteen specially constructed tracks propelled with the help of eleven hydraulic pulleys. What made the whole operation particularly complicated was the fact that the large building was not moved straight forward but at an angle of 78° to its original position. At present the residence serves as the Warsaw Garrison Club.

Front view

Pillared portico of the front elevation

Side view of the portico

The Lubomirski Residence (also known as the Szuster Residence) UL. PUŁAWSKA 55/57

This residence was built between 1772 and 1774 by Efraim Schroeger for Princess Lubomirska. Originally it was a villa in neo-classical style situated in gardens laid out by Szymon Bogumił Zug in the Mokotów estate. The basement was arranged into resplendent baths and the rest of the building was occupied by reception rooms. Rooms on the southern side of the villa were lower, leaving space for a mezzanine floor where a small suite was situated. All rooms were appointed with utmost luxury and excellent good taste.

In 1791 Szymon Zug changed the eastern elevation to the symmetric arrangement it has preserved to this day. When the princess died in 1816, Mokotów passed to her daughter, Aleksandra, married to Stanisław Kostka Potocki, connoisseur and patron of the arts, Minister of Education and Religious Denominations in the government of the Kingdom of Poland. In 1820, Aleksander Potocki, son of Stanisław, divorced his first wife, Anna, née Tyszkiewicz, and offered her Mokotów in return for sums she had spent on decorating their mansion of Natolin. Anna was very fond of the villa and restored it to its original splendour. In 1825, she had the western and northern elevations altered to neo-gothic style. It is believed she commissioned Henryk Marconi to do the work. Both elevations have been preserved to this day without major alterations. The Mokotów property was purchased in 1845 by the well-known Warsaw lithographer Franciszek Szuster. The residence was enlarged on two occasions during the latter half of the 19th century, a two-storey annex being added after 1865. Set on fire by enemy bombs in September 1939, the building burnt down. In the 1960s, it was restored by Jerzy Brabander and his team to the aspect it had at the end of the 19th century. The residence now houses the Warsaw Music Society.

View from the drive

View from the Vistula

Detail of the elevation facing the Vistula

The Małachowski Residence UL. SENATORSKA 11

In 1731, Józef Benedykt Loupia, mayor of Warsaw Old Town, bought terrain extending from Krakowskie Przedmieście to Senatorska Street. On this site he had a residence built in late baroque style, in line with Senatorska Street. In 1750, Jan Małachowski, Lord High Chancellor of the Crown, purchased the property from the Loupias; he had the residence enlarged and embellished, presumably according to Jakub Fontana's design. The chancellor's son Mikołaj sold the property in 1784 to the Rezler and Hurtig Company who soon built a large three-storey apartment house in the courtyard designed in neo-classical style by Szymon Bogumił Zug. The front of this building was on Krakowskie Przedmieście Street. Annexes were added, which joined the apartment house with the residence, ever since forming an inseparable whole. The property changed hands repeatedly in the course of the 19th century. When in 1888 Miodowa Street was extended to Krakowskie Przedmieście, the residence and the apartment house both acquired new side elevations. The residence burnt down in September 1939 as a result of enemy bombing. It was rebuilt in 1947, according to plans by Zygmunt Stępiński, save for the left annex which was demolished in order to leave open the view on the front elevation. The building now houses the offices of the Central Board of the Polish Tourist Society.

Elevation facing Senatorska Street

Elevation facing Miodowa Street

Palace of Ministers of Finance

This palace came into existence betwen 1825 and 1830 as a result of fundamental reconstruction of the former baroque Ogiński residence, according to plans by Antonio Corazzi. It was destined to serve as the residence of the then Minister of Finance, Prince Ksawery Drucki-Lubecki. Corazzi converted the building in renaissance style, modelling it on Italian villas. The general impression of Italian influence is intensified by large terraces, seldom found in the climatic conditions which prevail in Poland. The residence, like all buildings designed by Corazzi, was notable for its excellent proportions and arrangement of the different elements. Between 1919 and 1921 it was painstakingly restored according to plans by Marian Lalewicz, to serve as the Ministry of Finance. Like so many other buildings, it burnt down in enemy bombing in September 1939. The work of reconstruction continued from 1950 to 1954, under the direction of Piotr Biegański; together with the neighbouring Palace of the Government Revenue and Finance Commission, it was destined to serve as the seat of the Presidium of the Warsaw People's Council. At present, the palace also houses the Warsaw City Office. In 1951, a statue of Feliks Dzierżyński, designed by Zbigniew Dunajewski, was erected in front of the building. Two memorial plaques were set in the wall of the ground floor arcades: the first commemorates meetings of the Jacobin Club held in the Ogiński residence at the close of the 18th century, the second is in honour of Antonio Corazzi and was unveiled on 26 April 1977, the centenary of the death of this great architect.

General view from Dzierżyński Square

First floor room

The Młodziejowski Residence
UL. MIODOWA 10, UL. PODWALE 7/9

Also known as the Bidziński, Morsztyn or Igelström residence after the names of its consecutive owners, this building was already in existence in the latter half of the 17th century. We know what it looked like at the time thanks to an inventory dating from 1705, preserved in the National Museum in Stockholm. It was a two-storey building in late baroque style, topped with a hipped roof. The main entrance faced Podwale Street and was situated in the central projection which was surmounted with a pediment, rising above the rest of the building. The façade on the Miodowa Street side was designed more elaborately. It had a central projection identical with the one on the Podwale Street side, as well as two side projections, each surmounted by a pediment. A small symmetrically laid-out garden, closed with a wrought-iron railing, separated the residence from Miodowa Street. It is not known exactly when the residence was built or who designed it. It changed hands several times until in 1766 it was bought by Andrzej Młodziejowski, Bishop of Przemyśl. Młodziejowski carried out a fundamental conversion of the residence between 1766 and 1771, presumably according to designs by Jakub Fontana. The two side projections on the Miodowa Street façade were extended to form proper wings, which enclosed a courtyard separated from Miodowa Street by an arcaded gallery supporting a terrace. In his *Historical and Statistical Description of the City of Warsaw*, Łukasz Gołębiowski mentions that an ornamental tent used to be unfurled on this terrace, under which Bishop Młodziejowski took his luncheons or dinners, while observing the busy bustle in the street below.

The bishop, who eventually became Chancellor of the Crown, was certainly no ordinary personality. Coming from a modest gentry family, he owed his later dignities to his own wit and intelligence only, and his familiarity with matters of policy. Ruthlessly bent on accumulating money, he became famous for accepting bribes. Ultimately, he compromised himself by appropriating a large part of the estate left by the abolished Jesuit Order. His career began when he became chaplain to the papal nuncio. During that period he had an amusing adventure, recounted in his *Memoirs* by Bishop Ludwik Łętowski: "The Papal Nuncio used to pay a visit regularly once a week to Madame Zamoyska, wife of the Palatine of Lublin, with whom he was wont to partake of hot chocolate after Mass at the Capuchin Church. One week, being indisposed, or perhaps engaged on official business, he sent his chaplain to convey his compliments to the Lady and make his excuses. When the chaplain was announced the chocolate was ready and waiting to be served. 'Sit you down my good father,' said the Lady graciously, 'and have some chocolate.' Not daring to refuse, the chaplain did as he was bid, then paid his hasty respects and took precipitate leave only just in time for he was violently sick, ridding himself of what he had swallowed all over the staircase. By some inexplicable mishap, the servants had dropped Hungarian soap in the brew. The poor chaplain, having never tasted chocolate before, swallowed the horrible staff, thinking it was the concoction destined for the nuncio."

Młodziejowski contributed to the election of Stanislaus Augustus to the throne of Poland, thanks to which he enjoyed the king's favour. Like many other Princes of the Church of that period, the Bishop of Przemyśl had a paramour. The lady of his choice was Madame Drzewiecka, wife of the king's chamberlain. One night when the bishop, disguised as a lacquey, was returning home from a visit to his lady-love, he was stopped and arrested by a police patrol. News of the mishap which had befallen the bishop made the round of Warsaw drawingrooms immediately and Młodziejowski's ill repute spread beyond the country's frontiers, as the bishop had occasion to discover during the visit he paid to the great French philosopher and moralist, Jean Jacques Rousseau. When Rousseau heard the name of his visitor, he turned his back on him. Młodziejowski died in 1780. Three years later, Franciszek de la Riviere Załuski, Starost of Grójec, purchased the Miodowa Street residence from the heirs of the unfortunate bishop. In the 1790s, the residence was occupied by General Joseph Andreyevitch Igelström, commander-in-chief of Russian troops in Poland. During the Kościuszko Insurrection fierce fighting took place round the palace on 17 and 18 April 1794; Igelström made good his escape and left Warsaw in a great hurry. During its storming by troops under Jan Kiliński, the residence was destroyed. Acquired by Feliks Potocki, it was rebuilt between 1806 and 1808 in late neo-classical style. The work was put in the hands of Fryderyk Albert Lessel, who added two wings to the building on the Podwale Street side between 1808 and 1811. In 1818, the residence was bought by Karol Zeydler, and for a time housed the Warsaw Merchants' Club. During the 19th century, the building gradually lost its artistic merit, becoming a rented apartment house. Hit by enemy bombs in September 1939, it caught fire and was completely burnt down. It was rebuilt according to plans by Borys Zinserling in 1957. As a result, the building was restored approximately to its appearance after its reconstruction by Bishop Młodziejowski. The arcaded gallery which separated the courtyard from Miodowa Street was not rebuilt. At present the building houses offices of the State Scientific Publishers.

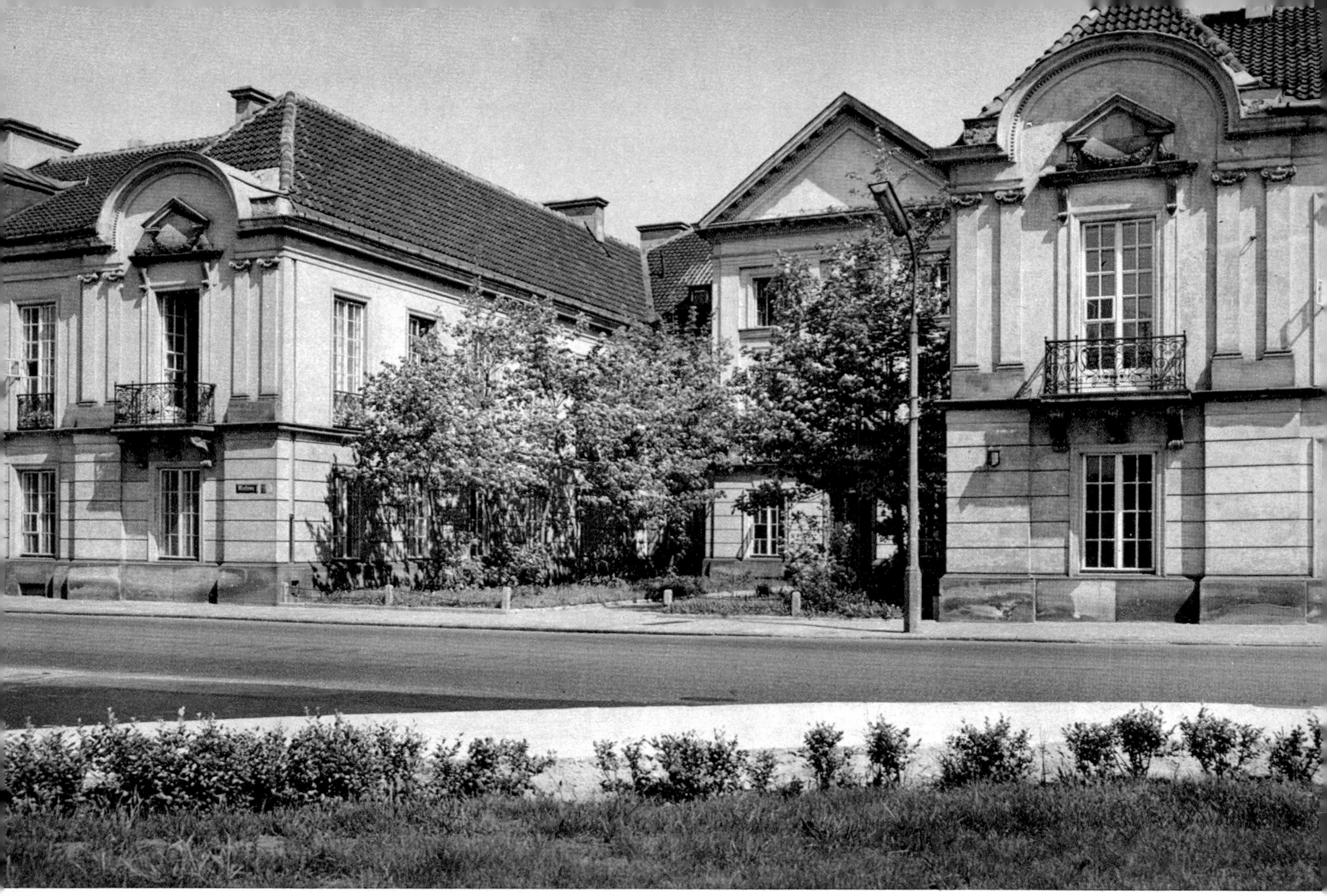

View from Miodowa Street

Front elevation from the Podwale Steet side with the armorial bearings of Bishop Młodziejowski

View from Podwale Street

The Mniszech Residence

UL. SENATORSKA 38/40

The site on which this residence was built was acquired by Józef Wandalin Mniszech, Lord High Marshal of the Crown, in 1714. Work on the residence, which exists to this day, began the next year. In 1716, Burchard Christoph von Münnich was placed in charge of construction. The same architect was probably responsible for the design of this late baroque residence which consists of the main building and two wings forming a large court-of-honour. Before 1762, the residence underwent alteration according to plans by Pierre Ricaud de Tirregaille, who included its view in this new aspect among other views shown on the border of his famous plan of Warsaw. In 1790, Józefina Potocka, née Mniszech, sold the residence to Prince Stanisław Poniatowski, Lord Treasurer of the Grand Duchy of Lithuania, who ceded it that same year to the banker and industrialist Prot Potocki. Later, the residence passed to Katarzyna Kossakowska, née Potocka, who gave it in 1801 to Jan and Feliks Potocki. The two Potockis used only the main body of the residence; they sold the wings and the gardens at the back. After the fire of 1805, the Potockis sold the main body of the residence to a Prussian official, Frederick Wilhelm Mosqua. The new owner restored the building and arranged a concert hall in it. The residence also housed the Harmonia Music Society founded by Ernst Theodor Wilhelm Hoffmann who lived on the premises. In 1829 the residence was acquired by the Merchants' Club, and that same year underwent fundamental reconstruction in neo-classical style, according to designs by Adolf Schuch. Up to 1944 the building remained the property of the Merchants' Club which held there meetings, lotteries, lectures and balls. During the Warsaw Uprising, it was turned into a hospital. Burnt down by the Germans, the Mniszech residence was restored after the war according to designs by Mieczysław Kuźma. It is occupied by the Belgian Embassy.

View shown on the border of the plan of Warsaw drawn by Pierre Ricaud de Tirregaille, 1762

Front view

The Mostowski Palace

UL. NOWOLIPIE 2, UL. NOWOTKI 15

Between 1762 and 1765, Jan Hilzen, Palatine of Minsk, acquired the site on which the Mostowski Palace now stands, and after dismantling the manor-house which had belonged in turn to the Pac family, the Bishops of Vilna, the Ponińskis and Adam Brzostowski, built himself a residence there. In 1795, the residence passed to his grandson Tadeusz Mostowski, Castellan of Raciąż, who sold it to the government of the Kingdom of Poland in 1822. In 1823, it was completely reconstructed and enlarged according to plans by Antonio Corazzi, to serve as the Government Commission of Internal Affairs and Police. Its monumental neo-classical facade features an imposing projection with an Ionic four-columned portico, decorated with sculptures attributed to Paweł Maliński and Aleksander Jan Norblin. After the Warsaw Uprising, the residence was destroyed by the Germans. Rebuilt and enlarged in 1949, according to designs by Zygmunt Stępiński, the building now serves as the Warsaw Headquarters of the Citizens' Militia.

Front view

Detail of the front elevation

The Pac Palace ul. MIODOWA 15

This residence was built for Prince Dominik Radziwiłł, from 1681 Deputy Chancellor and from 1690 Lord Chancellor of the Grand Duchy of Lithuania. The exact date of its completion remains unknown, but it was certainly finished before the chancellor's death in 1697. This building became the main body of the later residence designed in baroque style by Tylman van Gameren.

After the death of Dominik Radziwiłł, the residence passed to his heirs. Between 1744 and 1758 it belonged to Andrzej Załuski, Bishop of Chełm, later Bishop of Cracow and Lord Chancellor of the Crown. From the bishop's heirs, the property was purchased in 1759 by Michał Kazimierz Radziwiłł, nicknamed Rybeńko (his favourite saying which could be translated as 'odds fish'), Palatine of Vilna, through whom the residence returned to the Radziwiłłs. Between 1762 and 1775, it was rented by Prince Michał Fryderyk Czartoryski, Lord Chancellor of the Grand Duchy of Lithuania. In that period, King Stanislaus Augustus was a frequent visitor there. On 3 November 1771, as the king left the residence to drive back to the Royal Castle, the coach was stopped by Bar confederates who abducted king out of the city. The plan of abduction failed, however, for one of the conspirators had second thoughts and facilitated the king's escape. After spending the night in an old mill in Marymont, His Majesty returned safe and sound next morning to the Royal Caste.

Later, the residence was bought by Ludwik Pac who immediately undertook its fundamental restoration according to plan by Henryk Marconi. The reconstruction was completed in 1828. Marconi added wings on both sides of the court-of-honour and another building which closed it from the Miodowa Street end. The problem was that the main building faced Miodowa Street at an angle which upset the general layout. Marconi coped with this difficulty in a masterly manner. He adorned the front building with a semi-ellipsoid recess with two coachgates and a niche in the centre. The right-hand gate, facing the main body of the residence, led to the court-of-honour, whereas the left-hand one opened into a small circular yard. A frieze in bas-relief over the gates facing Miodowa Steet, sculptured by Ludwik Kaufman, matched the whole composition perfectly. It showed the Roman Consul Titus Flaminius proclaiming the freedom of Greek cities at the Games in Corinth. The exterior of the palace was given neo-renaissance and late neo-classical finish, while in the interiors, alongside of the neo-classical, also gothic and Moresque elements were used. Among the reception rooms, special attention should be drawn to the grand hall on the first floor of the main building, modelled on the Baths of Caracalla in Rome. Behind the residence Marconi built large semi-circular stables closing the palace gardens.

Finishing work on the interiors was interrupted in 1830 by the outbreak of the November Insurrection. For participating in the rebellion Ludwik Pac had all his estates, including his Warsaw residence, confiscated by the Russian authorities. From 1849, the residence was taken over by Russian government offices. Between 1876 and 1939, it housed the Warsaw District Court. Dur-

96

ing the interwar period, the palace underwent restoration which eliminated the various changes and alterations introduced by the Russians. The residence was destroyed during the Warsaw Uprising in 1944. Rebuilt between 1947 and 1951 according to plans by Henryk Białobrzeski and Czesław Konopka, it has been the headquarters of the Ministry of Health and Social Welfare ever since. The garden façade has regained its Tylman van Gameren style, while the front elevation of the main building and the house along Miodowa Street, both were restored to the appearance designed by Henryk Marconi. The Pac Palace is the last magnate residence in the history of Warsaw architecture.

Central part of the front wing

View form E-W Thoroughfare
The former Ballroom

The former Chapel

The Pod Blachą (Tin-Roofed) Palace

It will be guessed easily that this residence got its name from the roofing. Its history began in 1651, when the armourer, Wawrzyniec Reffus, began to build himself a house on land granted him by King John Casimir, immediately adjoining the Royal Castle. The house was certainly finished by 1656, and a year later was destroyed in the storming of Warsaw by troops under Stephen Rakoczy, Duke of Transylvania, during the Swedish wars. Work on rebuilding this house must have dragged endlessly, since it was not finished in 1687. In 1698, the building was bought by Krzysztof Montwid Białłozor, Canon of Vilna and Secretary to His Majesty, who ceded use of it shortly after to Prince Jerzy Dominik Lubomirski, Lord High Steward and later Lord High Chamberlain of the Crown. Lubomirski converted the building giving it a palatial western façade and adding a southern wing. He purchased the property in 1720 and shortly after undertook its further transformation. The palace acquired a late baroque appearance which it has preserved on the whole to this day. A northern wing was added and a spacious court-of-honour was formed. The residence was immortalised in this condition in two paintings by Bernardo Bellotto, called Canaletto, executed in 1772 and 1773.

The palace remained in the Lubomirskis' hands until 1776 when it was sold to the merchant Henri Colignon. On 4 August the following year the property was acquired by the king, who included the residence among the Royal Castle buildings; that same year the king commissioned Dominik Merlini with conversion of the interiors to serve as apartments for eminent courtiers. About that time, two storeys were added to the northern wing which then connected with the Royal Library built between 1780 and 1784.

In 1794, the king gave the residence to his nephew, Prince Joseph Poniatowski, who lived there between 1798 and 1806. At the time, Warsaw was part of the Prussian partition zone. Prince Pepi, as Joseph Poniatowski was affectionately called, led a turbulent style of life. He kept a sumptuous court, dominated, both in this residence and at Jabłonna near Warsaw, by his lady friend, the Countess Henrietta de Vauban, a French émigrée. The lady was not popular with Warsaw society. Kazimierz Władysław Wójcicki wrote that "the prince's close friends used to call her 'the old parrot' and in fact she led the life of a pet parrot in a golden cage. She was always complaining of indispositions, always suffering from the vapours, and simply could not abide fresh air; even at the height of summer she seldom went anywhere otherwise than by closed coach, and in the winter almost never left her overheated rooms. She would touch nothing but the daintiest of choice dishes, which were the curse of the prince's unfortunate chef. She could not stand the slightest noise, anybody approaching her had to step on tiptoe and speak in low tones; squeaky shoes were simply anathema. It was incredible how that spoilt, peevish mood-ridden Frenchwoman managed to rule the prince's whole retinue, but more incredible still was how she got great Polish ladies, whether residing in Warsaw or on temporary visits, to submit to her whims, almost without exception. Things reached a point where if she had to pay a return visit to one of the ladies who were regular visitors at Prince Pepi's, Madame de Vauban would drive to the lady's residence, send a footman with her card begging to be excused because the state of her health did not permit her to leave the carriage, and saying she would be pleased if the lady would graciously visit her in the carriage. And incredible to say, those grand ladies would run happily down from their magnificent apartments for a chat with the Vauban in her carriage. Such occasions became known as visits à la Comtesse de Vauban." The whole of Warsaw was kept wondering what on earth Prince Pepi could see in that "tall, thin, much-lived and by no means beautiful Frenchwoman", Wójcicki wrote. One thing was certain, she exploited the prince's infatuation mercilessly, extorting large sums of money from him under every pretext. The prince died hero's death in the Battle of the Nations only a few days after Napoleon had made him Marshal of France. The residence was inherited by his sister Teresa Tyszkiewicz, who sold it to the Tsar Alexander I in 1820. Various offices were then located in the residence. Between 1850 and 1854 it was completely restored by Gustavo Corri; the roof over the main building was lowered considerably. After the First World War, the residence housed the Ministry of National Defence and later the Central Military Library and the Administration of State Libraries. In 1924, the writer Stanisław Przybyszewski was granted a "grace and favour" apartment in the southern wing. The palace underwent fundamental restoration between 1932 and 1937 according to plans by Adolf Szyszko-Bohusz. The high roof of the residence was restored and covered with sheet-copper. All the façades were painstakingly renovated. Wishing to give back to the residence the aspect it had before 1777, Szyszko-Bohusz had the two storeys, added by Dominik Merlini to the northern wing, dismantled.

The residence escaped damage in September 1939, but save for part of the wings it was burnt down by the Germans during the winter of 1944. Rebuilt in 1948–49 according to plans by Stanisław Baran, the palace now houses the offices and studios of Warsaw's chief architect.

Front view

Detail of the central front elevation

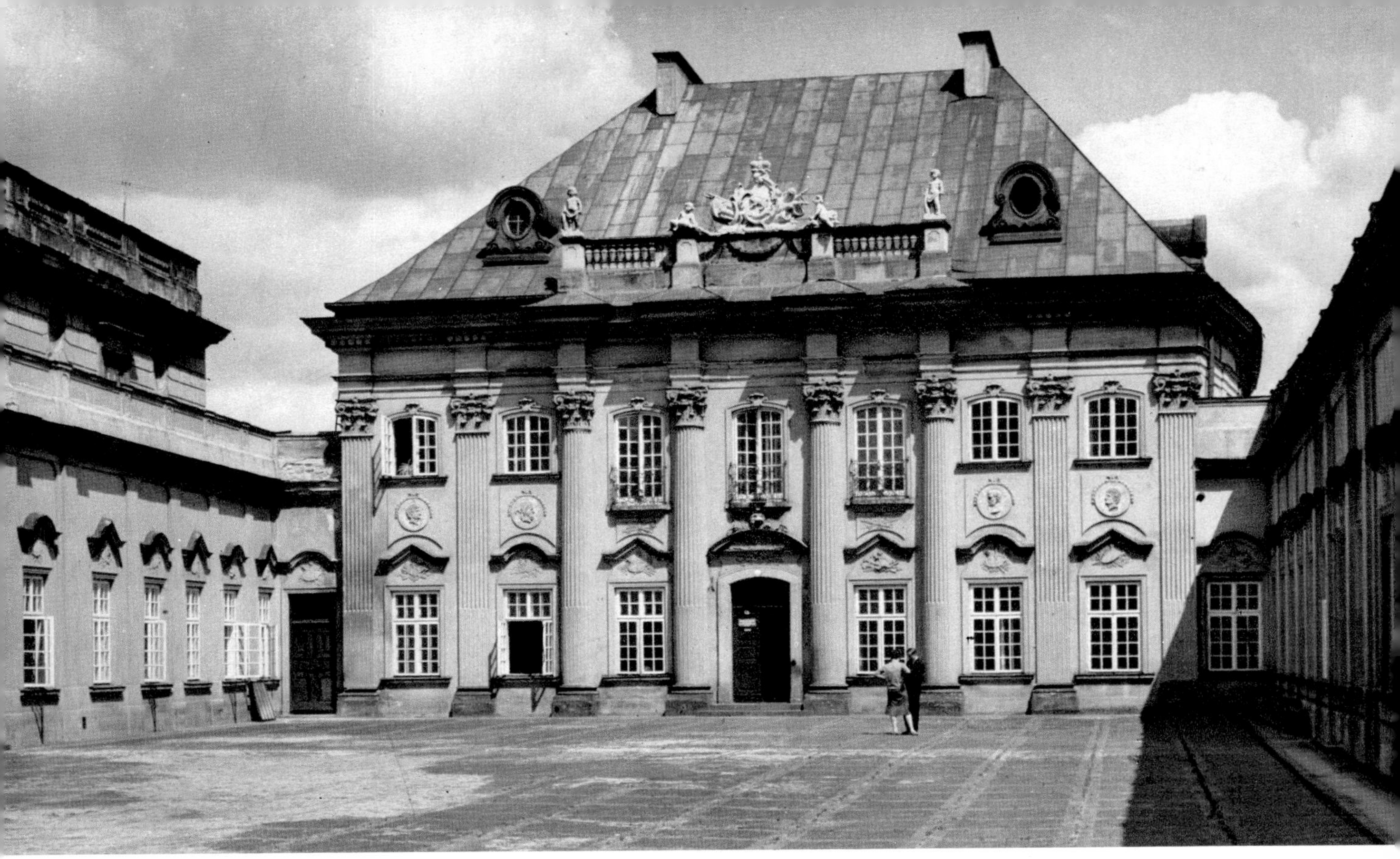

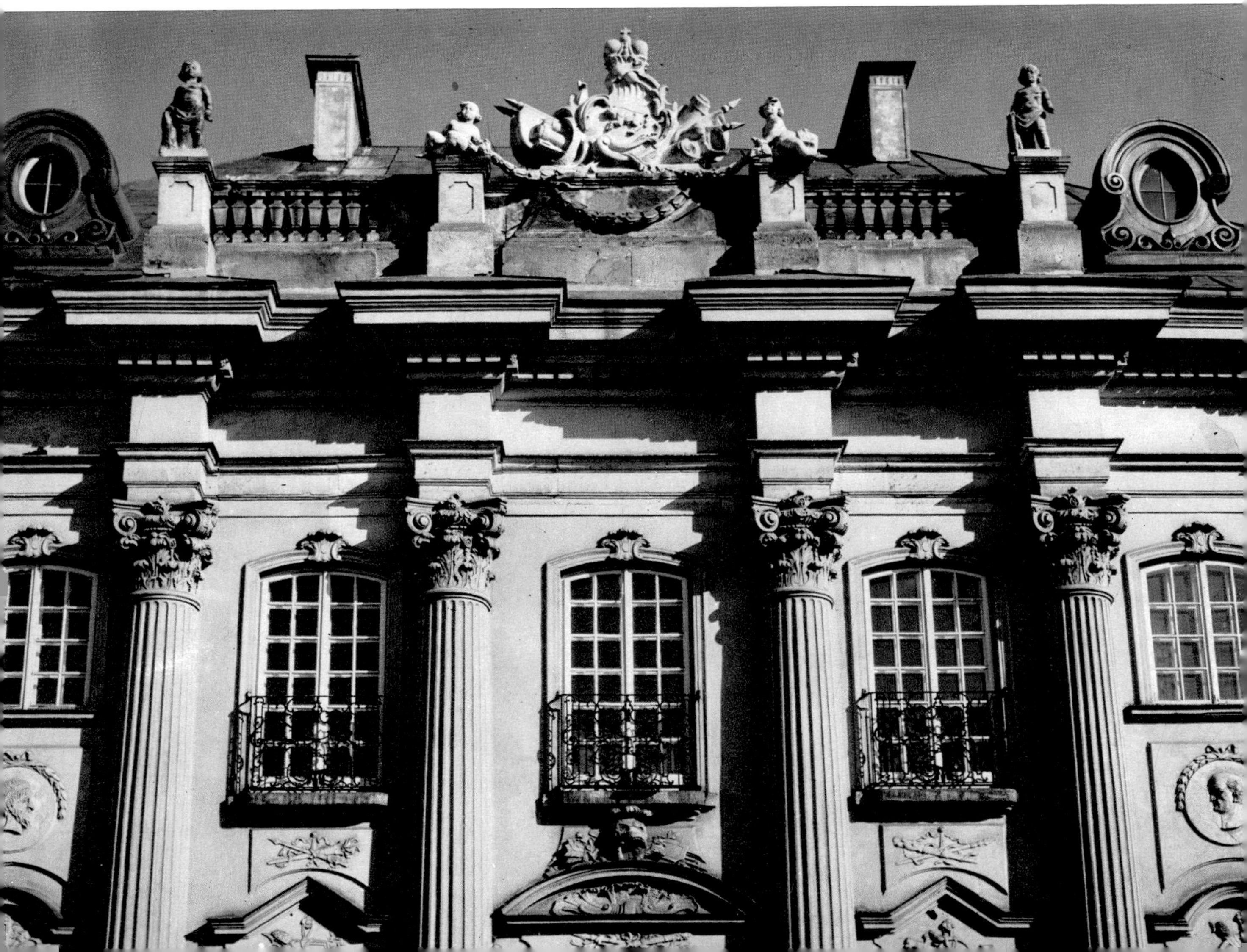

View from the Vistula

The Palace Pod Czterema Wiatrami (at the Four Winds) UL. DŁUGA 38/40

This residence owes its name to allegorical figures representing the four winds which adorn pillars of the railing separating its courtyard from Długa Street. It is also sometimes referred to as the Dückert Residence, after one of its 19th century owners. It was built by Stanisław Kleinpolt, who, after his ennoblement by the Seym in 1676, assumed the name Małopolski; he was record-keeper of the Crown Treasury, one of the king's secretaries, finally steward and standardbearer of Bracław province. Work on the residence began probably about the year 1680, certainly well before 1685, when it was acquired by Jan Dobrogost Krasiński, Referendary of the Crown and Starost of Warsaw. Krasiński did not use the residence very long, mainly because it was situated in the vicinity of the newly built splendid Krasiński Palace; in fact, he sold it in 1698 to Andrzej Załuski, Bishop of Płock. What is known of its late 17th century appearance is that it had a central body and two wings and was at least in part designed by Tylman van Gameren

The residence changed hands repeatedly in the course of the 18th century. About the middle of that century, the central projection of the main body was altered into rococo style. Between 1769 and 1771, the banker Piotr Tepper had important work done to the residence according to plans by Szymon Bugumił Zug. The right wing was enlarged and an annex was added to it at the Długa Street end, distinguished by an early neo-classical front. Zug is also presumed to be the designer of the square pavilions at the street end of both wings or at least of the extra floor added to them. About 1784, Zug prepared plans for a complete conversion of the interiors. It is believed that the large diningroom on the first floor, with a semi-circular ending, dates from that time.

The residence was sold in 1801 to the merchant Karol Fryderyk Dückert and until 1891 remained in the Dückert family. During the 19th century it was turned into a rented apartment house. Acquired by the State Treasury in 1927, it underwent fundamental restoration to serve as the seat of the Ministry of Labour and Social Welfare. The building was burnt down by the enemy action during the Warsaw Uprising in 1944. It was rebuilt in 1953 and at present houses the offices of various institutions subordinate to the Ministry of Health and Social Welfare.

105

General view

Central projection of the main building

The Potocki Residence

From 1643 on a manor-house belonging to the Denhoff family occupied the site where the residence now stands. Historians suggest that this manor-house was destroyed during the Swedish invasion. A new manor-house, in unpretentious baroque style, was built in 1693 by the architect Giuseppe Piola. In 1728, on the death of the then owner, Stanisław Denhoff, the property was inherited by his wife, Maria Zofia Sieniawska, who a year later, after the death of her mother, was left the entire vast fortune of the Sieniawski family, thus becoming the greatest heiress, probably in the whole of Europe. She had many suitors among ruling foreign princes and members of the highest Polish aristocracy. Finally, her choice fell on Prince August Aleksander Czartoryski, Palatine of Ruthenia, whom she married in 1731. The huge fortune his wife brought onto the Czartoryski house laid the foundations of that family's subsequent power.

The Czartoryskis did not undertake any major work on their Krakowskie Przedmieście property until about the year 1760, when the former manor-house was substantially enlarged and given an exterior in a mixture of late baroque and rococo styles. The well-known French architect Pierre Ricaud de Tirregaille showed the façade of the new palace on the border of his famous plan of Warsaw, executed in 1762. Shortly after, two side wings were added, forming a court-of-honour of imposing proportions. The Corps-de-Garde in rococo style facing Krakowskie Przedmieście, which exists to this day, was built between 1765–66. The name of the architect who was commissioned with all work is unknown, but the Corps-de-Garde is attributed to Efraim Schroeger. A number of well-known artists were employed embellishing the residence, among them the sculptors Samuele Contessa, Jan Chryzostom Redler and Sebastian Zeisel. Zeisel made the sculptures on the Corps-de-Garde. When the work was completed, the Czartoryski residence was unquestionably one of the most magnificent noble residences in Warsaw.

Following the death of August Aleksander Czartoryski in 1782, the residence passed to his daughter Izabella, married to Prince Stanisław Lubomirski, Lord High Marshal of the Crown. On her instructions, some of the rooms were converted to neo-classical style, according to plans by Szymon Bogumił Zug. Alteration of the façade of the main body in discreet neo-classical style and addition of the portico at the front entrance, supporting the first floor terraced balcony, attributed to Zug, is believed to have been done in 1790. The architect Jan Chrystian Kamsetzer and the painter Antonio Tombari contributed to the work of redecoration carried out in 1790 and 1791. In 1799, Izabella Lubomirska gave the Krakowskie Przedmieście residence to her daughter Aleksandra. After the latter's death in 1831, this mansion, as well as Wilanów, passed to her son Aleksander who reserved the main body of the residence for his personal use, and instructed that the remainder was to be rented. Gradually this aristocratic residence was turned to profit. The wing along Czysta Street, now Ossolińskich, was let out as shops; from 1857, the pavilion at the corner of

Czysta Street and Krakowskie Przedmieście housed the famous Gebethner and Wolf bookshop and publishing firm. The court-of-honour was leased to Gracjan Unger, who in 1881 built a large exhibition pavilion there, according to plans by Leandro Marconi. In 1886, Józef Potocki of Antoniny acquired the residence, and in 1896 set about its complete restoration. The Unger pavilion was dismantled. Neo-baroque forged-iron gates, designed by Leandro Marconi, were fitted on either side of the Corps-de-Garde. Władysław Marconi, Leandro's brother, was put in charge of the work of restoration. Following Józef Potocki's suicidal death in 1922 the residence passed to his elder son, also Józef. The building did not survive the Second World War; on 7 August 1944, at the beginning of the Warsaw Uprising, the Germans poured petrol all over the residence and set it on fire. Rebuilt shortly after the war, according to plans by Zygmunt Stępiński and under the supervision of Jan Zachwatowicz, it is now occupied by the Ministry of Culture and Art.

View shown on the border of the plan
of Warsaw drawn by Pierre Ricaud de
Tirregaille, 1762

A bird's eye view of the Potocki Residence *(bottom)* and
the Palace of the Council of Ministers *(above)*

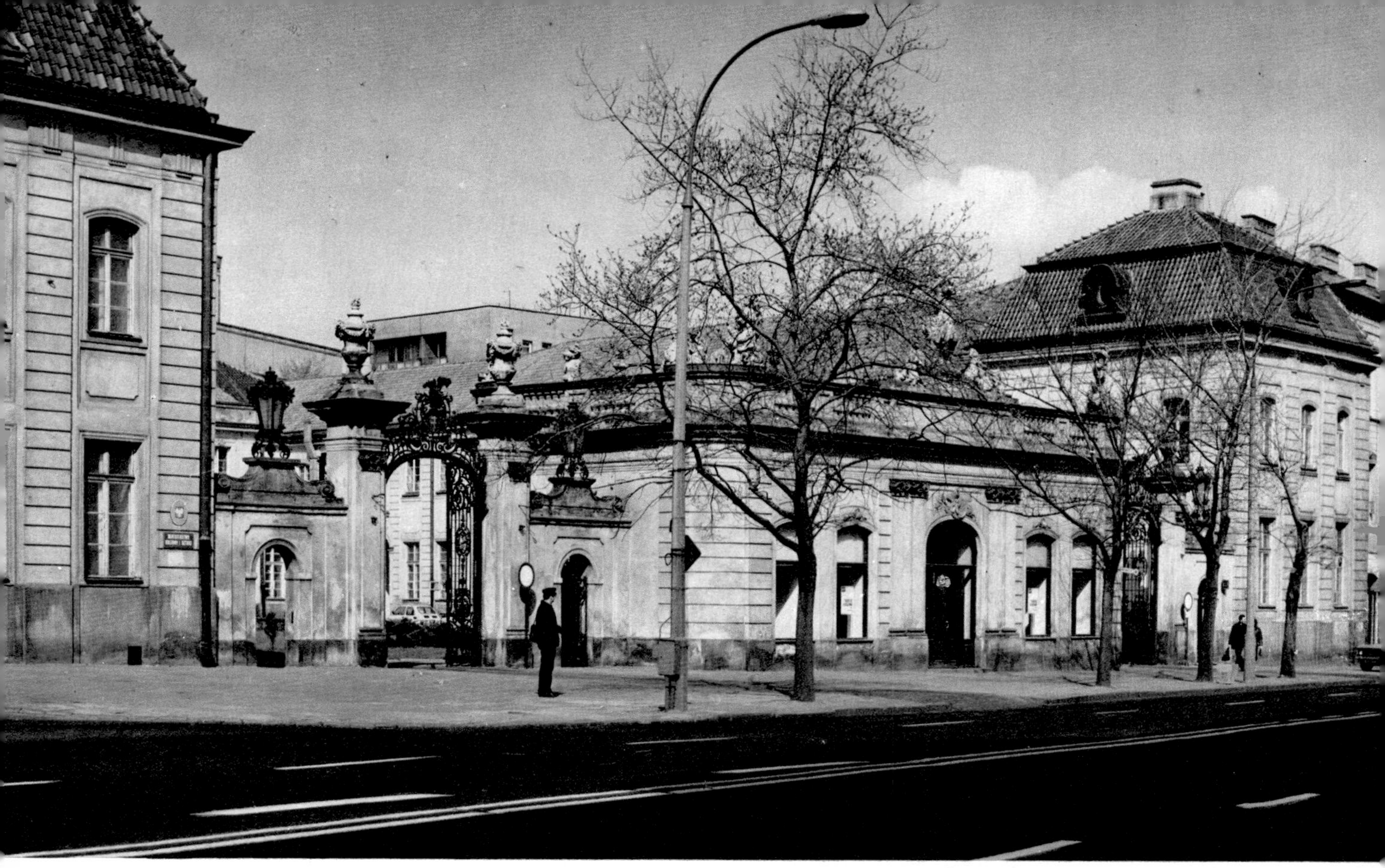

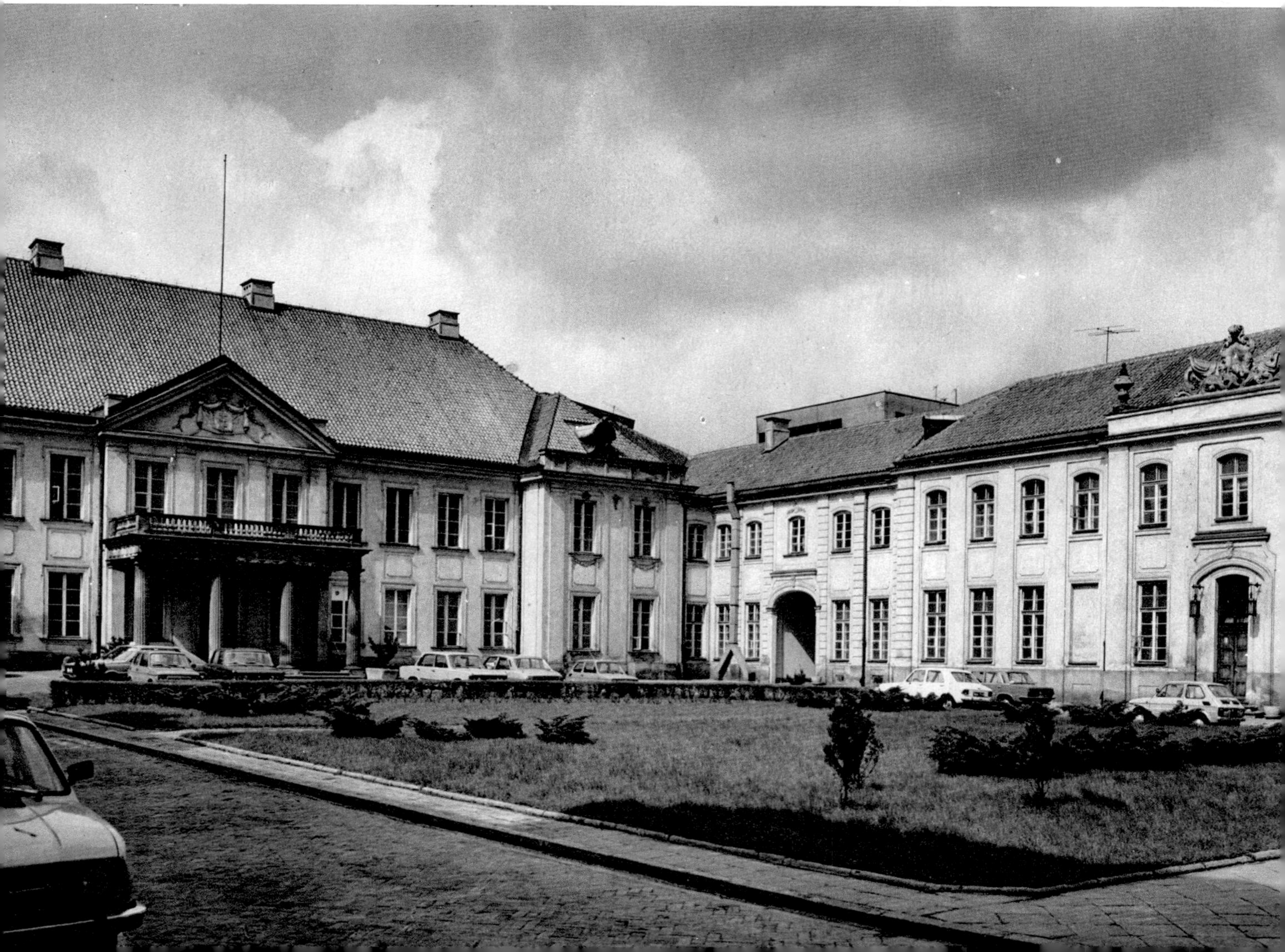

General view from Krakowskie Przedmieście Street

The main building and the right wing

The gate

The Potocki Residence at Jabłonna

Jabłonna, a place situated on the right bank of the Vistula, lies less than twenty kilometres from the capital. In the 15th century it came into the possession of the Bishops of Płock, who eventually chose it for their summer residence. Prince Charles Ferdinand Vasa, son of Sigismund III and brother of Ladislaus IV, Bishop of Wrocław and Płock, had a private chapel built here in 1646, "in the building which served relaxation among friends, after toils and duties", states a marble memorial plaque in the northern face of the present residence. Nothing is known of that chapel or of the episcopal residence which stood there in those days.

In 1773, Michał Poniatowski, brother of King Stanislaus Augustus, future Primate of Poland, became Bishop of Płock. That same year he purchased Jabłonna from the Płock Chapter, and the next year, began its conversion into a modern palatial residence standing in extensive parkland. In 1774, work also began on a new residence for the Bishops of Płock, according to plans by the court architect Dominik Merlini. The whole project, including the laying out of the park, was completed in the mid-1780s.

The mansion consisted of a single-storeyed main building and two square three-storeyed side annexes. The right-hand annex attached another rectangular two-storeyed outhouse. The main building was roofed in 1775, but work on its decoration was still continuing in 1777. The architecture of the building was in baroque style, whereas its décor and ornaments were neo-classical. The front elevation was adorned with a rectangular turret topped with a dome and globe. The garden elevation had a large three-sided projection inside which a circular drawingroom was situated. The main entrance led through a rectangular vestibule situated in the central projection of the front elevation. The vestibule opened on the circular drawingroom, connecting with two rectangular, oblong shaped three-windowed rooms, of which the right one was a diningroom and the left one a conservatory. On either extremity small suites were situated, consisting of a bedroom, dressingroom and bathroom. This arrangement remains virtually unchanged to this day, except that the northern suite was changed into one large room during a later conversion by Henryk Marconi.

The circular drawingroom, much higher than the other rooms, is certainly the most arresting of the apartments. Its walls are divided by composite pilasters supporting the substantial moulding on which a balcony rests. The ceiling features a painting by Szymon Mańkowski which shows blue skies on a sunny day besprinkled with small white clouds. The stucco ornaments are by the Italian artist Antonio Bianchi. Bianchi and Mańkowski also decorated other rooms in the residence. The basement rooms are covered with frescoes by Antonio Tavelli. The vaulted ceiling of the circular room directly under the drawingroom, rests on a central pillar painted with scenes of a satyr pursuing nymphs through woods and reeds. The main building was used by Bishop Michał Poniatowski, while the annexes and the outbuilding were reserved for the bishop's guests and his retinue.

The left annex is called the Royal Suite to this day, because it is said that Stanislaus Augustus used it when visiting his brother. In 1778 Szymon Mańkowski decorated it with grotesque paintings. The first-floor drawingroom is embellished with landscape paintings and the adjoining room with an allegorical scene showing the four seasons of the year in the guise of women of different races.

The English style park and its garden structures were designed by Szymon Bogumił Zug. The grotto, built about 1778, the neo-classical orangery built in the early 1780s and the Chinese Pavilion built in 1784, have been preserved to this day.

When Michał Poniatowski died in 1794, Jabłonna passed to his nephew, Prince Joseph Poniatowski, who intended to make it his permanent residence. After the third partition of Poland, however, he was forced to leave the country and settled in Vienna. On returning to Warsaw in 1798, he divided his time between his Warsaw residence, the Tin-Roofed Palace, and his country house of Jabłonna. Both residences were lorded over by the Prince's friend, Henrietta Comtesse de Vauban. Up to the year 1806, the prince led a gay revelling way of life, kept magnificent horses, a private band of musicians, entertained lavishly, spending far more than the revenue from his by no means negligible estates. In Jabłonna, Prince Joseph occupied the ground-floor suite of the right annex.

After the prince's heroic death at the Battle of the Nations in 1813, Jabłonna passed to his sister Teresa Tyszkiewicz, with the stipulation that on her death the property would go to her relative, Anna Potocka née Tyszkiewicz. The latter took possession of Jabłonna in 1822. After her divorce from Aleksander Potocki in 1821, she married the Napoleonic General Stanisław Dunin-Wąsowicz.

The new owner soon set about putting the residence in order. With the intention of turning Jabłonna into a centre of the cult of Prince Joseph, she had a triumphal arch built in the park in his memory. She assembled keepsakes and objects which had belonged to the prince or were in any way connected with that heroic figure.

A new gate was set up at the park entrance, with two granite pillars brought from Malbork Castle; picturesque cottages were built on either side of the gate bearing the inscription SALVE. In 1837, the residence underwent fundamental alteration according to plans by Henryk Marconi. New additions were built on either side of the central projection of the front elevation. The central part of the elevation was divided by Ionic pilasters, which radically altered its aspect. As regards the interiors, only the circular drawingroom was left as it was. The conservatory was given new cast-iron decorations in Mauresque style. A columned pergola was added to the northern end of the residence, which housed a collection of

Roman sarcophagi and sculptures. The façade was adorned with a plaque bearing the following inscription: "This Spot, Sacred to the Hero, Having Carefully Embellished It Without Touching Any of the Mementoes, I Hand Over To Descendant Generations. 1837. A.D.W.", with A.D.W. standing for Anna Dunin-Wąsowicz. A medallion over the inscriptions shows the figure of a seated woman sculptured in bas-relief. As regards the collection of ancient sculpture, items preserved to this day include a Roman medallion engraved with a bust of the Emperor Nerva, and a bas-relief sculpture by the Italian Renaissance artist Baccio Bandinelli, showing the bust of a bearded man, acquired by Anna Dunin-Wąsowicz during her travel in Italy in 1826–27.

Henryk Marconi also built farm buildings in Jabłonna, large stables and coach-houses.

Maurycy Potocki, younger son of Aleksander and Anna, was the next owner of Jabłonna. In 1879 the property passed to his son August, the Count Gucio mentioned at length below.

Jabłonna changed but little in the latter half of the 19th century. The outhouse adjoining the right annex was converted to serve the needs of the family. The anti-flood bank built along the Vistula at the end of the park spoilt its beauty by obstructing the view on the river. When August Potocki died in 1905, the property passed to his only son Maurycy, in whose hands it remained till 1945. The residence in Jabłonna burnt down in August 1944 as a result of enemy action. In 1945 steps were taken to preserve what remained of the building and in 1953 Jabłonna was handed over to the Polish Academy of Sciences, carefully rebuilt and restored to serve as a place where important conferences are held. Work of restoration was carried out by the Studios for Conservation of Historic Buildings and Monuments in Warsaw, according to plans by Mieczysław Kuźma and Gerard Ciołek.

The residence was not restored to its state in the time of Primate Poniatowski, or in the days of Anna Dunin-Wąsowicz. The central part of the front elevation obtained its 18th century appearance, but the additions built on either side of it by Marconi were preserved. As regards the interiors only the circular drawingroom was restored to its original state. The Mauresque ornaments of the former conservatory were beyond hope of repair, the damaged paintings in niches were restored and the room was finished in neo-classical style. The paintings and furnishings at present in the residence on the whole harmonize with the character of the restored building. Paintings by Tavelli in the basement rooms have been restored to their original brilliance. The Royal Suite now serves as a Club for Diplomats.

Front view

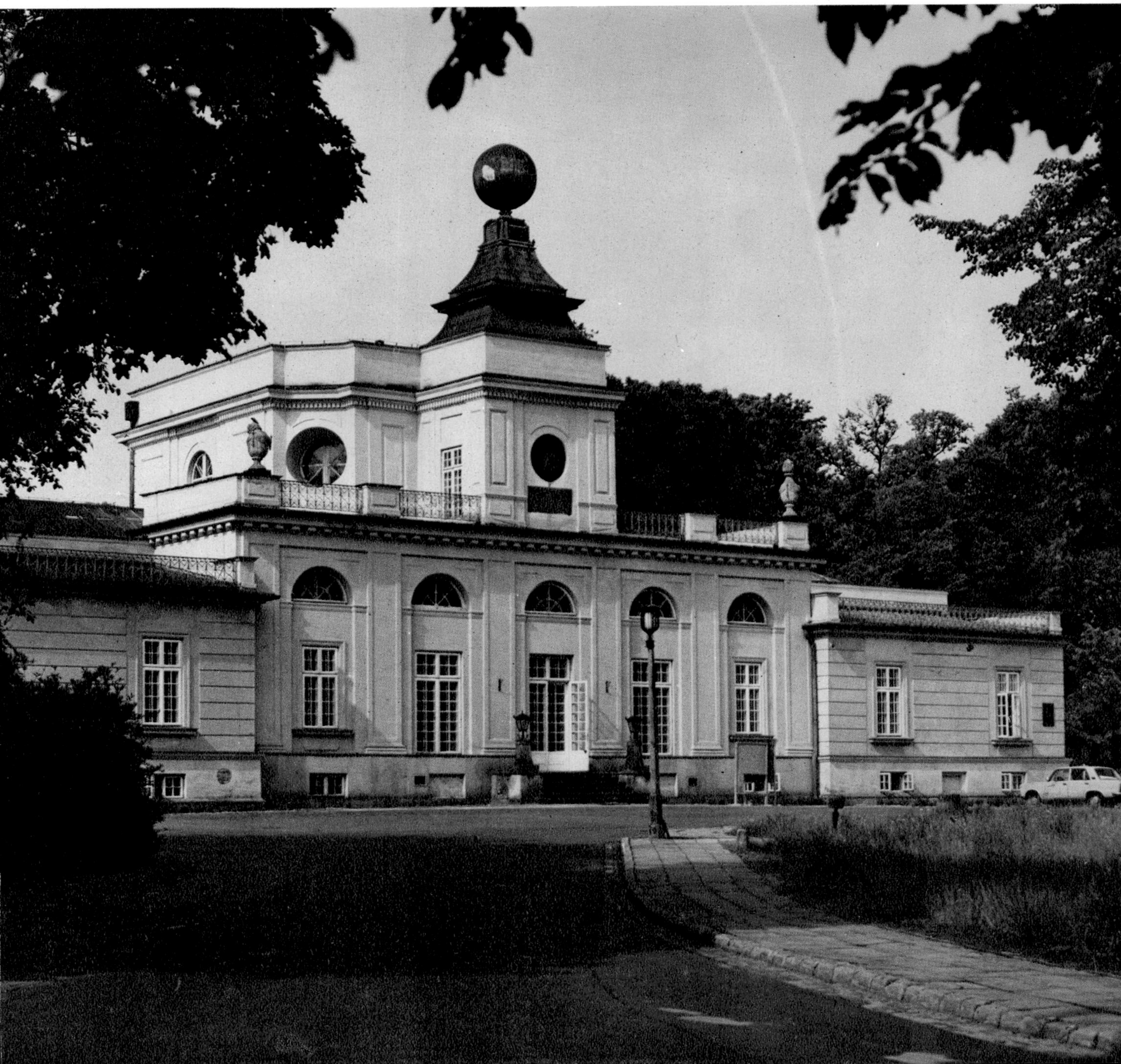

Garden view

Inscription over the entrance to the basements commissioned by Anna Dunin-Wąsowicz, née Tyszkiewicz

USTRONIE BOHATERA
OZDOBIWSZY STARAŃIE
BEZ NARUSZENIA PAMIĄTEK
POTOMKOM PRZEKÁZUIE
1837.
A. D.W.

The Circular Room

The Potocki Residence at Natolin

Natolin, originally a pheasantry on the Wilanów estate, is an attractive locality famed for the charming little residence built in the late 18th century on the edge of the former Vistula embankment in a large English style park. Between 1780 and 1783, Prince August Aleksander Czartoryski, owner of Wilanów at that time, had a small residence built there according to plans by Szymon Bogumił Zug. August Czartoryski died in 1782, the work was finished by his daughter, Princess Izabella married to Prince Stanisław Lubomirski, Lord High Marshal of the Crown, who received Wilanów as part of her dowry. The residence was built in the shape of a rectangle with two side projections jutting out at the front; the rear elevation facing the embankment had an Ionic colonnade on which the oval ground-floor drawingroom opened. This drawingroom and other rooms in the residence were decorated with frescoes painted by the Italian painter and architect Vincezo Brenna, specially brought over from Italy by Izabella's son-in-law, Stanisław Kostka Potocki. Brenna's frescoes were ruined when the residence was altered at the beginning of the 19th century. Princess Lubomirska took little interest in the Pheasantry, as the residence was then called. In 1787, she gave the use of it to her daughter Aleksandra and her husband Stanisław Kostka Potocki. When in 1799 the couple took over the whole of Wilanów estate, including the Pheasantry, Potocki busied himself with the redecoration of the Palace of Wilanów, whereas the Pheasantry was left neglected until the wedding of the Potockis son, Aleksander with Anna Tyszkiewicz in 1805, when it became their summer residence. When their daughter Natalia was born in 1817, the Pheasantry was renamed Natolin in her honour.

Work on the Pheasantry, which began in 1806, extended to its surroundings also. A two-storey annex in neo-classical style was built between 1806 and 1808; the layout of the park was altered; stables and a coach-house were built between 1808 and 1809; between 1810 and 1812 a great terrace was added along the edge of the embankment at the rear of the residence; between 1812 and 1814 a Dutch cowshed was built in a mixture of gothic and neo-classical styles in the lower park. In 1807 and 1808 the architect Chrystian Piotr Aigner was employed in Natolin. He designed the ornaments and décor of the interiors known as amphitheatres, the great ornamental vase on the terrace and a number of smaller ones set up on the terrace balustrade facing the embankment, and along the main drive; he also helped in designing the Dutch cowshed. Aigner is also believed to have designed the neo-classical lodges at the entrance gates to the grounds from the Wolica and Wilanów side, built in 1823.

Work of restoration and alterations to the residence, begun in 1806, at first only encompassed the front elevation, which was changed by introduction of Doric order; this spoiled the uniform style and composition of the four façades of the residence. The Doric frieze along the walls of the entrance-hall was added in the same year. These alterations were probably designed by Stanisław Kostka himself, who, among his many other talents, was also an amateur architect. The frescoes in the private suites occupied by Anna Potocka and her husband date from the same year.

The winter of 1807/08 was a turning point in the history of the ground floor rooms. The frescoes by Brenna were replaced with stucco ornaments designed by Piotr Aigner. Thus the newly appointed open drawingroom, reception room, mosaic cabinet and diningroom acquired a beautiful finish in mature neo-classical style characteristic of the beginning of the 19th century.

Anna and Aleksander Potocki were divorced in 1820, hence alterations carried out at Natolin after that date were due exclusively to Aleksander. The next major changes came between 1834 and 1838, when the statue of Natalia Sanguszko née Potocka, who died in 1830 was set up in the grounds of the Natolin Park. The statue itself is the work of the sculptor Ludwik Kaufman, whereas its pedestal is attributed to Henryk Marconi. Marconi also designed the Mauresque style bridge leading to the statue, the Doric Temple, Roman Aqueduct and Mauresque-Gothic Gate. Some of the first floor rooms were given a new décor between 1842 and 1845, including Anna Potocka's former suite which was arranged in Etruscan style.

Up to 1945 Natolin was part of the Wilanów estate whose owners, first the Potockis and later the Branickis, left it neglected. Garden structures and ornaments were not properly kept up, and those which became derelict were pulled down. The Dutch cowshed was dismantled immediately after the First World War. The last war did not spare Natolin. German troops quartered there during the Warsaw Uprising and after, devastated the residence and grounds. In 1945, Natolin was taken over by the Warsaw National Museum. Subsequently, the residence underwent general repairs and restoration, after which it was handed over for representative functions.

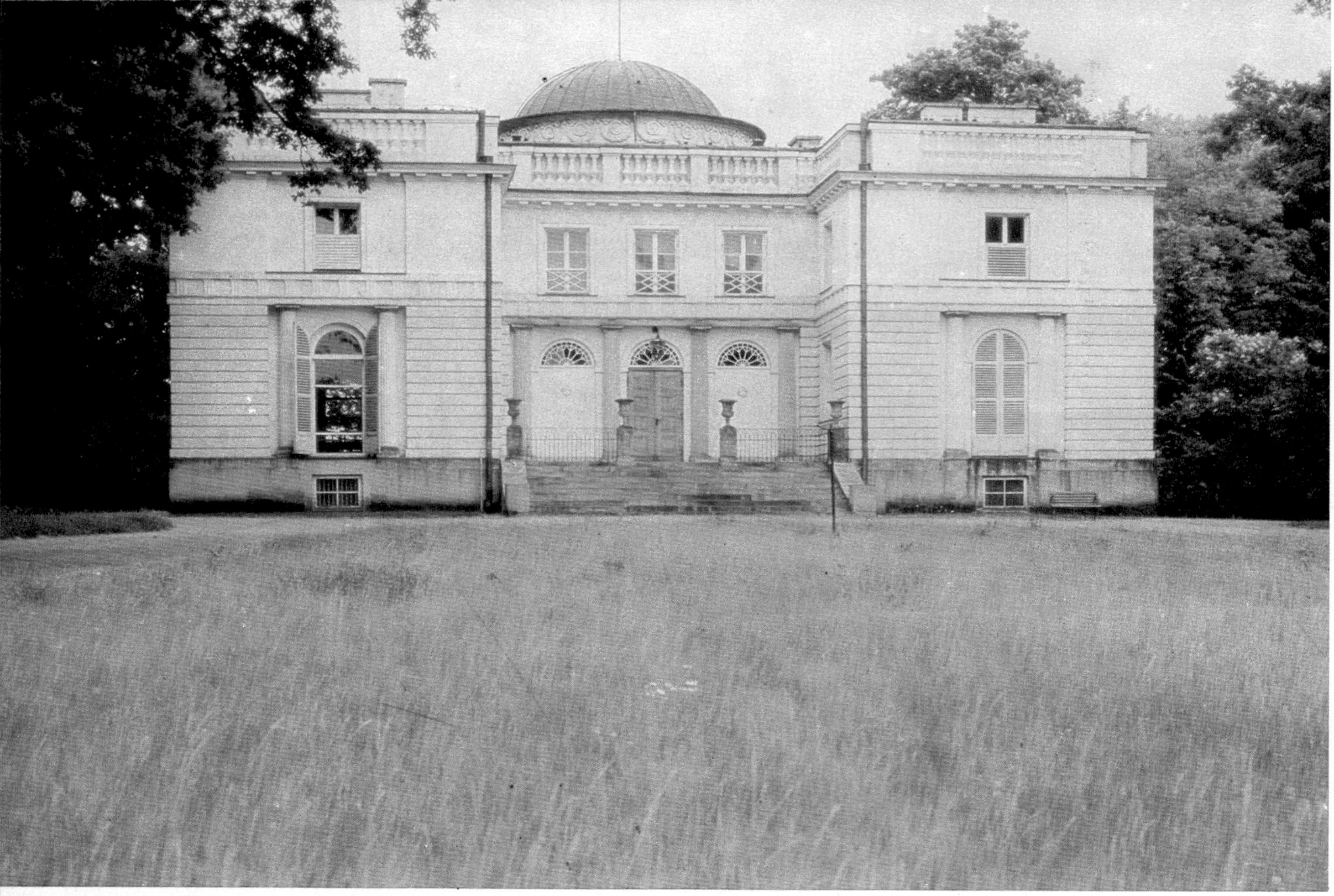

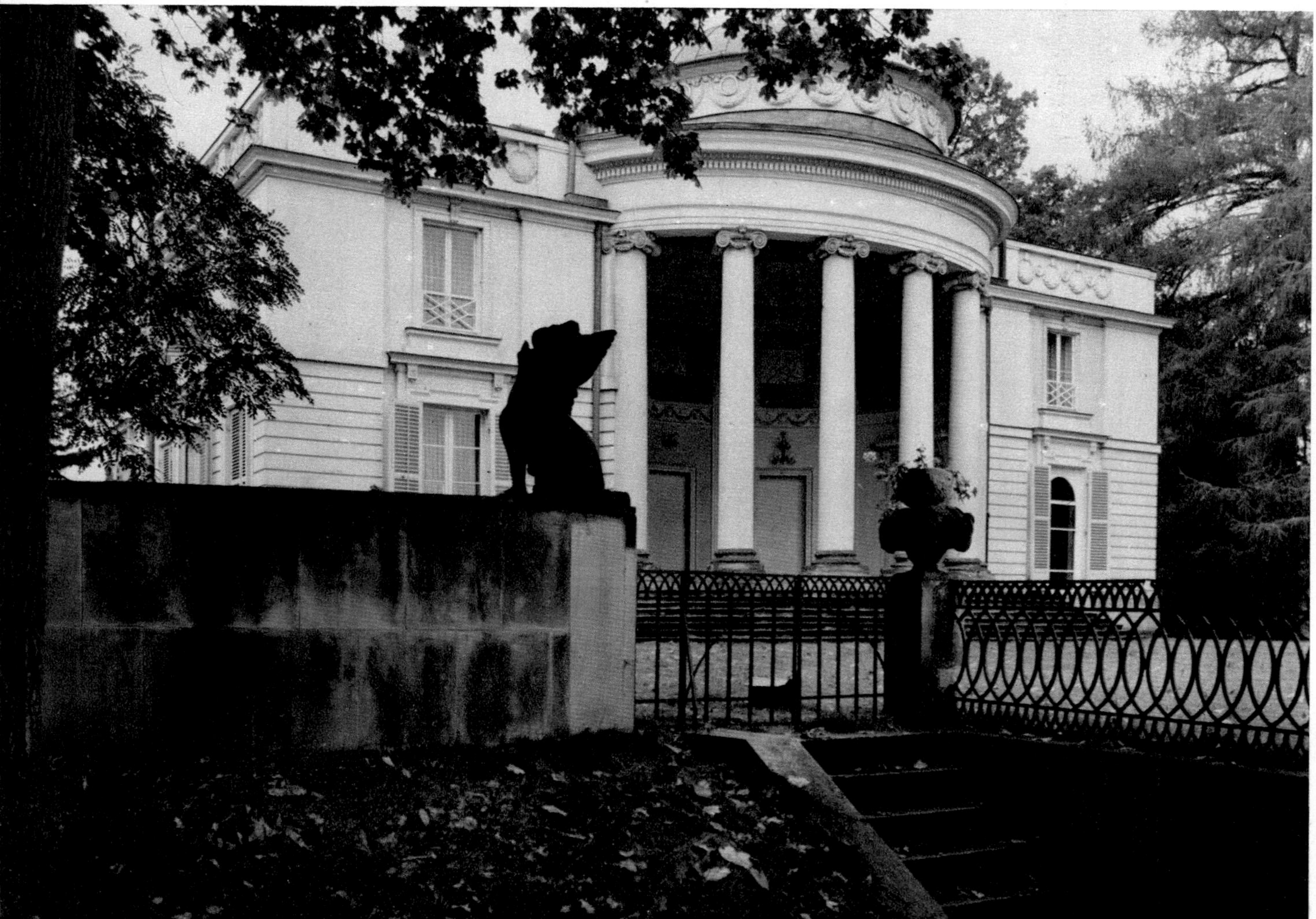

View from the drive
Garden view

The Mosaic Cabinet on the ground floor
The Etruscan Cabinet on the first floor

The Primates' Palace

UL. SENATORSKA 13/15

When Wojciech Baranowski, then Bishop of Płock, acquired this piece of land in 1593, with the intention of building a residence there for himself and his successors, it was occupied by various little houses and breweries. Nominated Archbishop of Gniezno and Primate of Poland, Baranowski changed his original intention and in 1612 bequeathed the palace to the Chapter of Gniezno Cathedral, with the stipulation that it was to serve as residence of the Primates of Poland. Work on the residence was completed by Primate Wawrzyniec Gembicki, and his successor, Primate Jan Lipski contributed to its embellishment. The palace, destroyed during the Swedish wars, was restored between 1666 and 1673 by Primate Mikołaj Prażmowski according to plans by Józef Fontana. The residence was enlarged and subjected to further work of restoration in 1690 and 1691 by Primate Michał Radziejowski, presumably according to plans drawn by Tylman van Gameren. During fighting between rival pretenders to the throne of Poland, Augustus of Saxony and Stanislaus Leszczyński, Augustus II occupied the suburbs of Warsaw in 1704; he gave free rein to his Saxon, Cossack and Wallachian troops to loot the palace of Primate Radziejowski, his political opponent, and they did a thorough job of it. The residence was restored by Primate Stanisław Szembek when the architect in charge of the work was Giovanni Battista Ceroni; decoration of the palace interiors was completed by Primate Teodor Potocki. The residence underwent basic reconstruction between 1749 and 1759, under Primate Adam Ignacy Komorowski, when it acquired a rococo finish. The aspect of the palace after this reconstruction was immortalised by Pierre Ricaud de Tirregaille on the border of his famous plan of Warsaw.

Large-scale reconstruction of the palace in neo-classical style was undertaken by Primate Antoni Ostrowski who entrusted the architect Efraim Schroeger with drawing up plans. Schroeger was also in charge of the work from 1777 until his death in 1783, when his place was taken by Szymon Bogumił Zug. The work, begun by Primate Ostrowski, was continued by his successor, Michał Poniatowski, brother of Stanislaus Augustus. Decoration of the interiors was placed in the hands of the court architect, Jan Chrystian Kamsetzer. As a result of all these alterations, a portico of four Ionic columns was added at the main entrance and extra height was given to the side projections by the addition of blind walls, leaving untouched the baroque hipped roof over the central part of the building. Two semi-circular wings connected the main body with pavilions featuring Doric porticos. Another pavilion in neo-classical style served as a magnificent ballroom. Many rooms were redecorated in neo-classical style, for example the Audience Chamber, the Yellow Room, the Mosaic Room and the Azure Room. On the first floor of the left wing, a splendid suite was prepared for Józef Oborski, Castellan of Ciechanów, Marshal of the Primate's court, and administrator general of towns belonging to the Archdiocese. Oborski owed his position to his beautiful wife, Petronela, née Ostrowska, the primate's paramour, who ruled unchallenged at the Tuesday receptions the primate gave regularly in his residence. She usually dressed in purples on these occasions to emphasize the closeness of her relations with this Prince of the Church. Primate Michał Poniatowski died in his Warsaw residence on 12 August 1794 in dramatic circumstances. A letter he addressed to the king of Prussia in which he indicated the weak points in Warsaw's defences, was intercepted during the Kościuszko Insurrection. Threatened with arrest, he took poison, which is said to have been supplied by his royal brother. Following the suppression of the Kościuszko Insurrection, Field Marshal Alexander Suvorov, the ruthless and blood-thirsty conqueror of the city, chose the Primates' Palace for his residence. When Warsaw was part of the Prussian partition zone, Minister Karl Georg Heinrich von Hoym resided there. In the Duchy of Warsaw the palace became a government property. During the Kingdom of Poland period, it housed the Government War Commission between 1816 and 1832. Later, it was occupied by the offices of various military institutions. After 1870, the building was taken over by a Russian military school, and later by the Administration of Military Engineering. The building was·repeatedly altered in the course of the 19th century; a floor was added to the main body which was a misconceived innovation. In 1927, the residence underwent another unfortunate adaptation, according to plans by Marian Lalewicz, to serve as the Ministry of Agriculture and Agrarian Reform. During the siege of Warsaw in September 1939, the palace was burnt down and destroyed by enemy bombs. Work on reconstruction of the building according to plans and under the supervision of Kazimierz Saski, was begun in 1949. The residence was intended to house the General Administration of Museums, Historical Buildings and Monuments. The palace, including some interiors, was restored to its state at the close of the 18th century. At present, it is occupied by various institutions subordinate to the Minister of Culture and Art.

View shown on the border of the plan of Warsaw drawn by Pierre Ricaud de Tirregaille, 1762

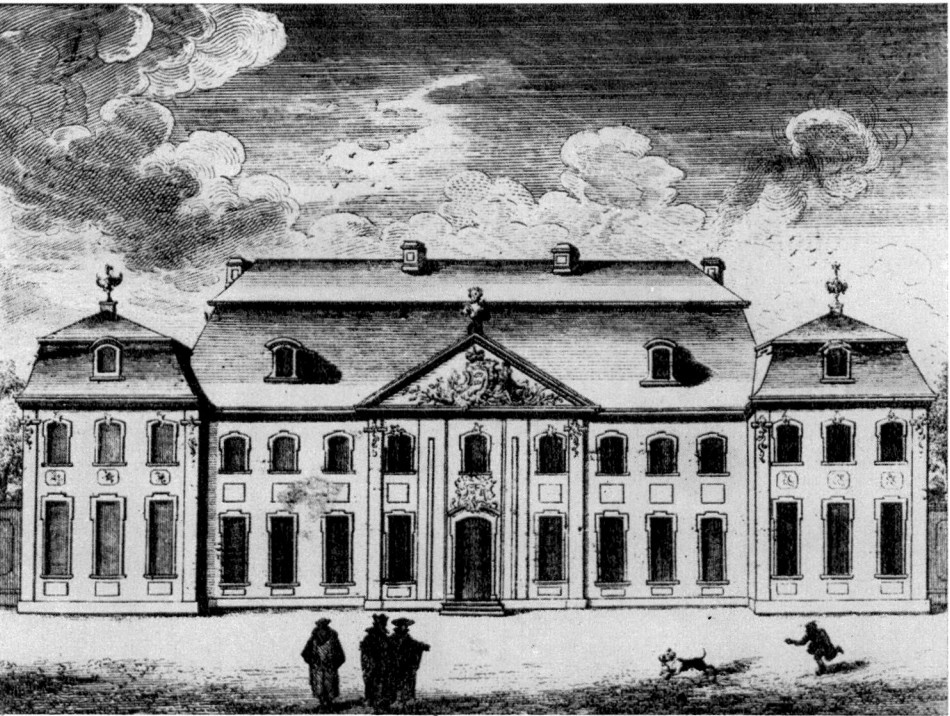

Main building

The Balroom

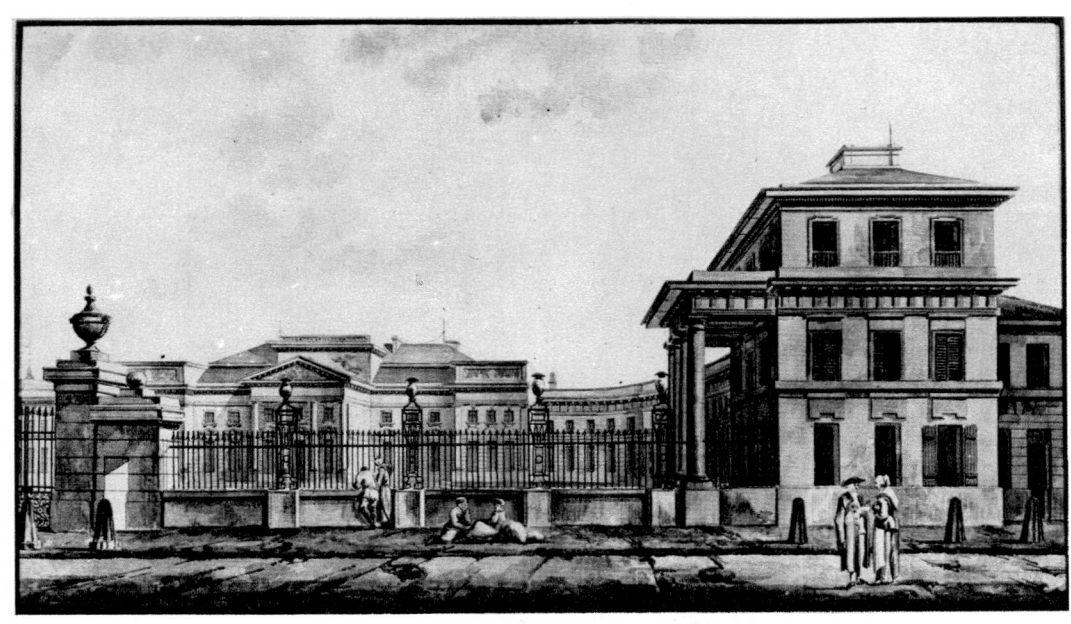

A view of the Primates' Palace by Zygmunt Vogel, 1789

General view

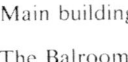

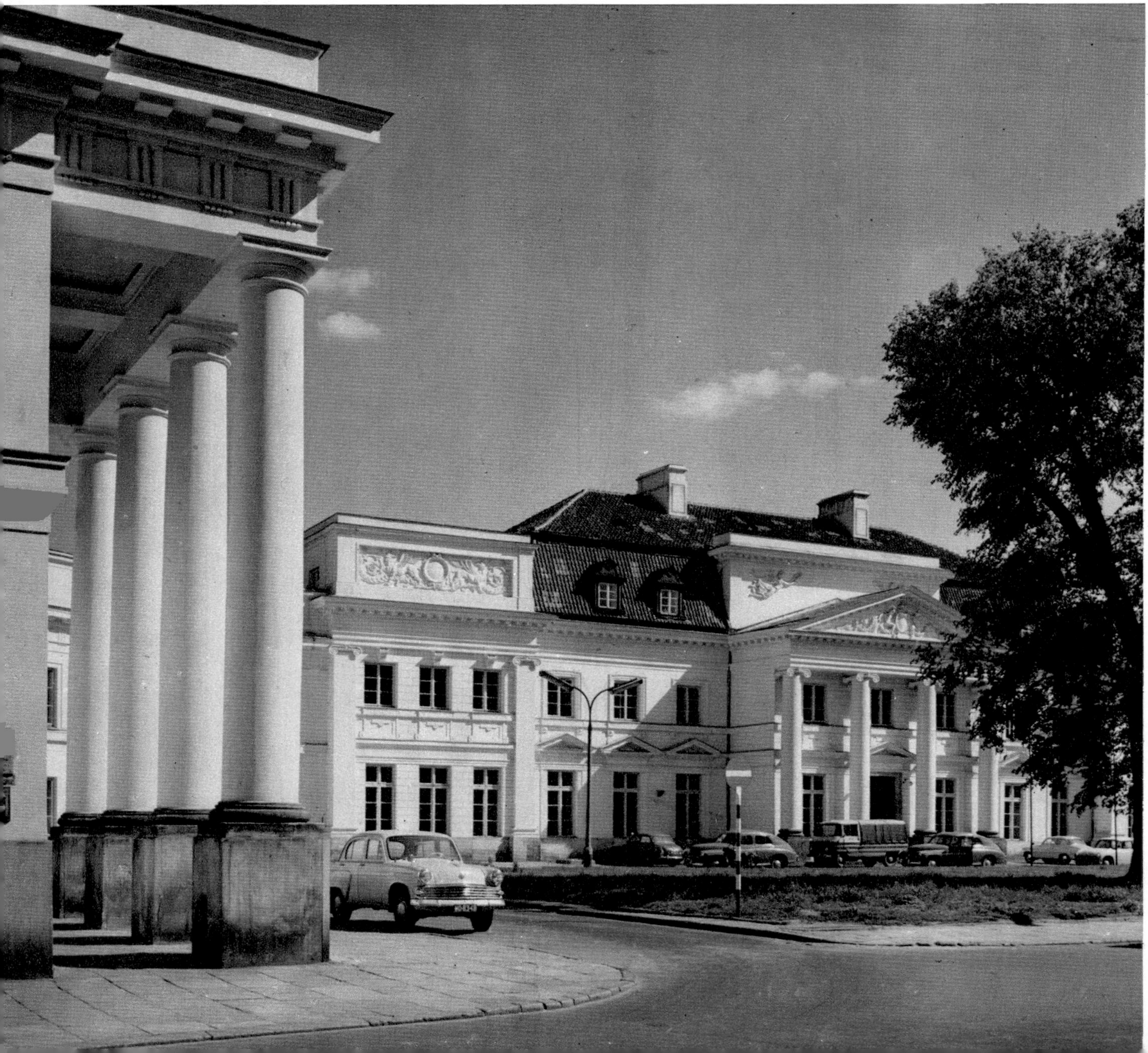

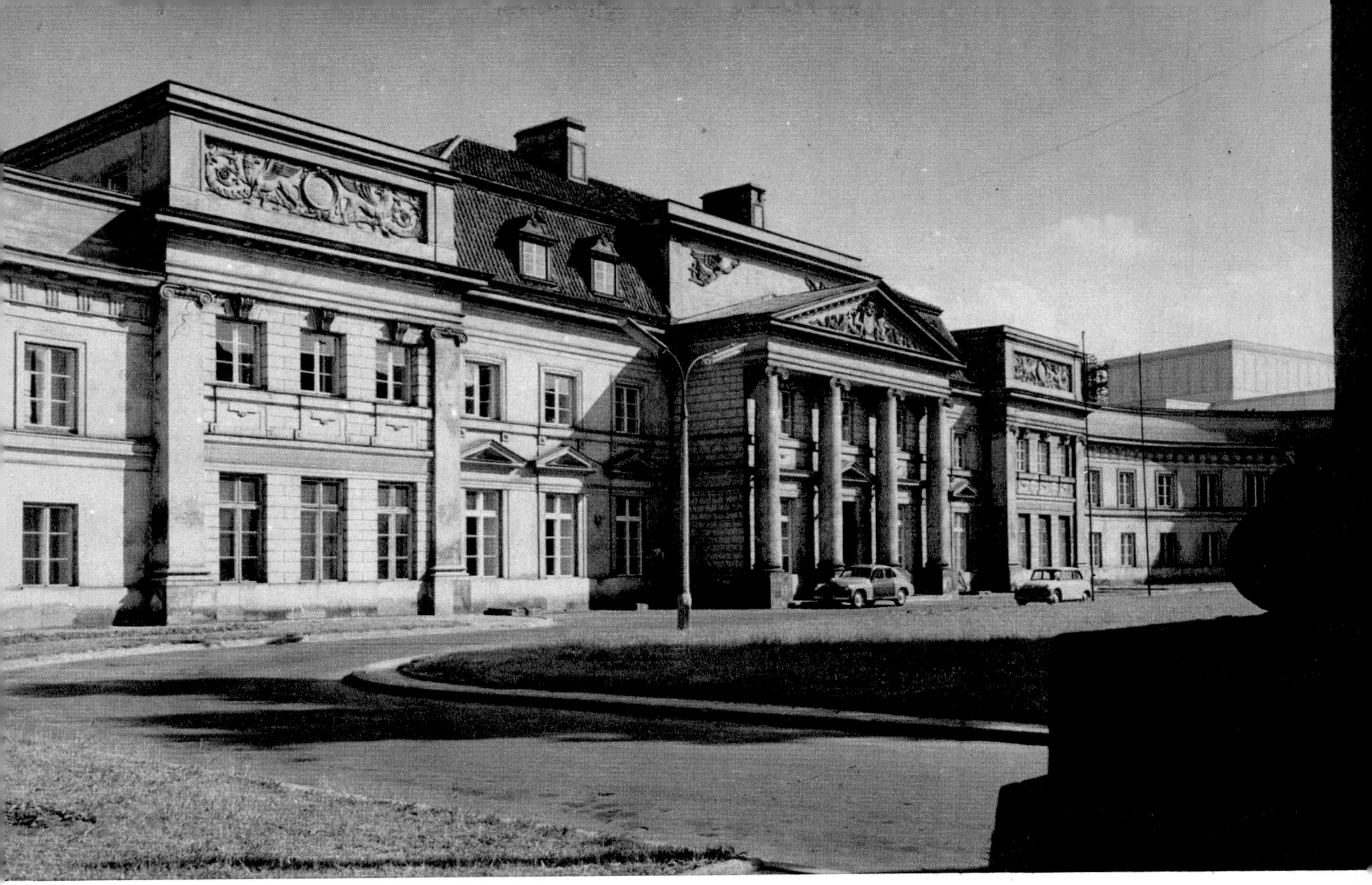

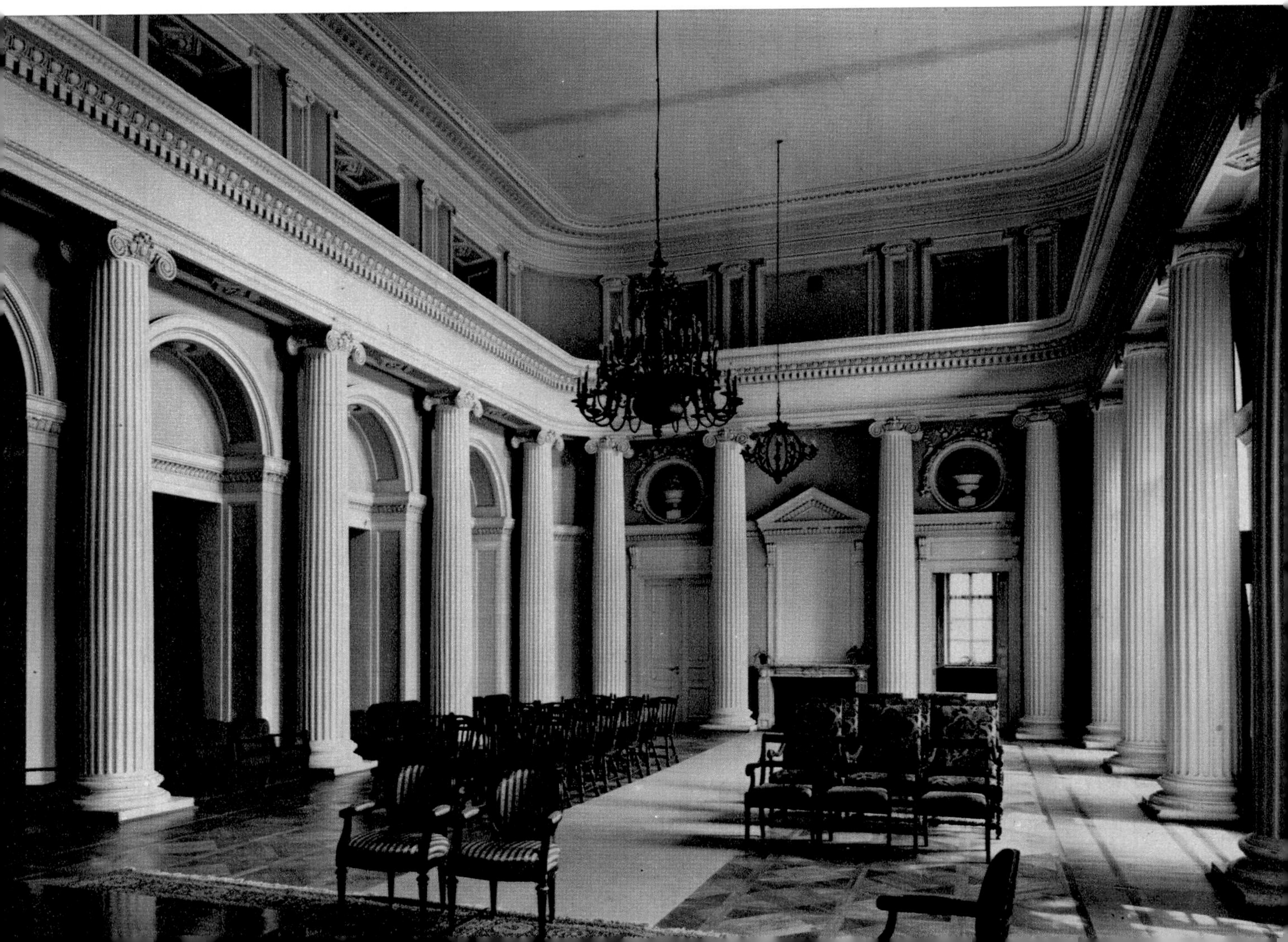

The Przebendowski Palace

UL. ŚWIERCZEWSKIEGO 62

Also known as the Zawisza or the Radziwiłł residence, after the names of its subsequent owners, this palace originally stood in Bielańska Street, but when the East-West thoroughfare was built, it was left on an island formed by this street. It was built in late baroque style before 1729 for Jan Jerzy Przebendowski, Lord Treasurer of the Crown, according to plans attributed to Jan Zygmunt Deybel. The property remained in the hands of the Przebendowski family till the end of the 1760s. It was rented by Pedro Pablo Abarca de Bolea Aranda, artillery general, diplomat and politician, who used it as his residence when he was Spanish envoy to the court of Augustus III, between 1760 and 1762. Aranda, an interesting colourful figure, subsequently contributed to the expulsion of the Jesuits from Spain. In 1780 Aranda founded the Masonic Lodge of Spain and became its first Grand Master. The magnificent receptions he used to give in the Przebendowski residence during his stays in Warsaw, became legendary.

At the end of the 1760s the property was acquired by Roch Kossowski, subsequently Lord Treasurer of the Crown. His second wife was Barbara, née Bielańska, famous for her charm and beauty, reputed to be one of the three most beautiful Polish ladies in the Stanislaus Augustus period – next to Rozalia Lubomirska, née Chodkiewicz, and Julia Potocka, née Lubomirska. Here follows a choice piece of scandal, of which those three ladies were the heroines, described by Stanisław Wasylewski, expert on the Stanislaus Augustus period: "Those three ladies, dressed in costumes befitting goddesses only, stole into Prince Pepi's bedchamber, and within the batting of an eyelid transformed it into a Mount Olympus, or perhaps Mount Ida. Then they hid behind a curtain and waited with beating hearts, each clutching a little present. At dead of night the dearest Pepi came at last, flushed, gay and sleepy, and what's more not alone, but in the company of... that common little actress Sitańska. Enfer et damnation!"

When in the hands of the Kossowski family, the residence underwent no major alterations. At a time when the whole of Warsaw of the Stanislaus Augustus period was changing its appearance, this residence preserved its late baroque style. It remained the property of the Kossowskis till 1831 after which it changed owners repeatedly. It fell into bad times in the first half the 19th century when it housed an exhibition of wax figures, a servants employment agency, an inn, a beer-house, a café and pastry shop, and a furniture store. It was acquired in 1863 by Jan Zawisza who immediately proceeded to restore the residence completely according to plans by Wojciech Bobiński. In 1883, Henryk Siemiradzki decorated the ceiling in the entrance hall with an allegorical painting representing *Light and Darkness*. Zawisza assembled a large archaeological collection in the residence. At the beginning of this century, the residence passed to Janusz Radziwiłł, one of the leaders of the Polish aristocracy and landed gentry between the wars, and remained in his hands until 1944. During the Warsaw Uprising, the residence was almost totally destroyed. Work of reconstruction began in 1947, according to plans by Bruno Zborowski, who restored to it its 18th century appearance. To begin with the building served as the training centre of the Central Trade Unions Council; since 1955 it has been occupied by the Lenin Museum.

Front view
Staircase

The Raczyński Residence

UL. DŁUGA 7

The history of this property goes back to the late 17th century, when it belonged to the Warsaw Alderman Jakub Schultzendorff, who commissioned Tylman van Gameren in 1699, to build him a residence stretching from Długa Street all the way to Podwale Street. This plan was never put into effect, though historians of architecture attribute to Tylman van Gameren the baroque house built there at the beginning of the 18th century, facing Długa Street. In 1717, the property was acquired by Konstanty Felicjan Szaniawski, Bishop of Kujawy, who enlarged and embellished the building to such an extent that it could aspire to the name of palace. After changing hands several times, in 1787 the residence was purchased by Filip Raczyński, a general of the Polish army. Shortly after Raczyński ceded the residence for life to his father-in-law Kazimierz Raczyński, governor-general of Great Poland and Marshal at the Court of Poland. The latter was one of the most despicable characters among the magnates of the time. He was an obedient servant of the Russian Embassy and enjoyed the favour of the Empress Catherine, which he knew how to turn to good profit. Hence it was not surprising that the Patriotic Party held him in contempt and ridiculed him. Warned at the very last moment, he made a hasty departure from Warsaw just before the outbreak of the Kościuszko Insurrection in 1794, thus avoiding the gallows he justly deserved.

Kazimierz Raczyński, an enlightened and highly educated man, connoisseur of architecture, immediately set about converting the baroque residence to neo-classical style. Work continued from 1787 to 1789 according to plans by the court architect Jan Chrystian Kamsetzer. An Ionic portico surmounted by a pediment was added to the front elevation in Długa Street; the interiors, above all the first floor reception rooms, were given a sumptuous neo-classical décor. Prominent among them was the magnificent ballroom, resembling the ballroom in the Tyszkiewicz Palace and that in Łazienki Palace, both designed by Kamsetzer. In 1810 the residence became the exclusive property of Atanazy Raczyński who sold it in 1827 to the government of the Kingdom of Poland, to serve the Government Commission of Justice. In 1853 and 1854 the annexes were restored according to plans by Alfons Kropiwnicki. When the Commission was closed down in 1876, the left annex was taken over by the Commercial Court, whereas the stately rooms on the first floor were occupied by the Russian president of the Court. Between 1919 and 1939, the palace housed the Ministry of Justice, during which time it underwent fundamental restoration under the supervision of Marian Lalewicz. A bas-relief sculpture representing the blindfolded head of Themis, the work of Mieczysław Lubelski, was added on the pediment of the Długa Street elevation.

During the Nazi occupation, the palace was taken over by the *Deutsches Obergericht,* or the supreme judicial authorities for occupied Polish territories. On 24 January 1944, the Germans lined up fifty Poles against the wall of the residence on the Kiliński Street side, and shot them. During the Warsaw Uprising, the residence was turned into a hospital, the largest in the Old Town, liquidated by the SS on 2 September 1944. Only fifty of the four hundred and thirty wounded in the hospital managed to make their escape; the rest were shot by the Nazis and the building was set on fire.

The residence was rebuilt between 1948 and 1950 according to plans by Władysław Kowalski and Borys Zinserling. It now houses the Central Archives of Historical Documents. The ballroom was rebuilt between 1972 and 1976.

Front view

Detail of the decoration of the Ballroom

Portico of the main elevation

The Ballroom

The Palace of the Council of Ministers

This residence is also known as the Koniecpolski or the Radziwiłł Palace and the Governor's Palace after its consecutive owners and occupants. Work on the main building of the residence was begun in 1643 and completed before the year 1655. The residence was founded by Stanisław Koniecpolski, Grand Hetman of the Crown, and designed probably by the Italian architect Costantino Tencalla. Between 1661 and 1685 the property belonged to the Lubomirskis and in 1685 it was bought by the Radziwiłłs. It was then a three-storey building in the shape of an extended rectangle with side projections at either end, standing on the high Vistula embankment.

The residence was reconstructed between 1694 and 1705 by Agostino Locci, Carlo Ceroni and Andrzej Jeziornicki and renovated again between 1720 and 1722 under the supervision of Karol Bay. Domenico Cioli, brought over from Italy in 1728 especially for the purpose, restored the ornamental grotto under the residence and eliminated damp which had attacked the foundations. The residence was reconstructed between 1755 and 1762 according to plans by Jan Zygmunt Deybel. Two wings were added at the front of the residence and the main building was altered to late baroque style. Pierre Ricaud de Tirregaille immortalized a view of this residence on the border of his plan of Warsaw executed in 1762. At the turn of the 18th century, the residence boasted a theatre arranged in the first floor ballroom.

In 1818, the residence was purchased from the Radziwiłłs by the government of the Kingdom of Poland, to serve as the residence of the governor, at the time General Józef Zajączek. It was reconstructed in neo-classical style in 1818-19, according to plans by Chrystian Piotr Aigner. Aigner extended the wings right up to Krakowskie Przedmieście. He also built a new grand hall and staircase in place of the old one, at the junction of the main body of the residence and its northern wing. He also transformed the front elevation in elegant academic neo-classical style, and the garden elevation in renaissance style. He altered and redecorated first and second floor rooms, leaving the ground floor virtually unaltered owing to the difficulty presented by the massive vaultings. The two-storey high ballroom situated on the first floor was the most magnificent of the rooms designed by Aigner. A number of prominent artists helped Aigner with the reconstruction and redecoration of the building, for example the Italian Camillo Landini, who sculpted the four stone lions guarding the court-of-honour in front of Krakowskie Przedmieście, and Nicola Monti, who decorated with paintings one of the ground floor rooms. Since then, the exterior appearance of the residence has remained virtually unchanged to this day, but not so Aigner's first and second floor rooms, which were almost totally destroyed by the great fire which broke out on 22 February 1852. Only the ground floor, protected by its massive vaultings, escaped damage. Restoration was carried out under the supervision of Alfons Kropiwnicki. Eight new allegorical figures by the sculptor Paweł Maliński were set up along the parapet, in place of the ones destroyed by fire. Two of the original figures escaped damage in the fire. The palace interiors were redecorated in 1856 according to designs by Bolesław Paweł Podczaszyński, specially for the visit of Tsar Aleksander II.

During the second half of the 19th century and the first decade of the 20th, the Russian authorities introduced many alterations to the interiors, built a number of cheap shoddy partition walls and new doors and openings between rooms, with complete disregard for their value as fine examples of period architecture. The grand hall on the ground floor was divided up into several small rooms, which ruined it completely. A statue of the loathed and detested Russian Governor Ivan Paskevich Erevan was set up in 1870 in the court-of-honour where it remained until 1917. Between 1918 and 1921, the residence was thoroughly renovated by Marian Lalewicz, who restored the interiors to their former condition. The palace became the seat of the Council of Ministers in independent Poland. The arrangement of some of the rooms was altered to adapt them to the new role; the interiors were in neo-classical style, harmonising with Aigner's architectural design. In 1924, the neo-renaissance building (No. 50 Krakowskie Przedmieście), reconstructed at the end of the 1870s by Józef Dietrich, was joined up with the northern wing of the residence. The palace sustained more damage during the German occupation when it was turned into a *Deutsches Haus*. After the war, it once again underwent thorough restoration between 1947 and 1952, supervised by Teodor Bursche, Antoni Jawornicki and Borys Zinserling.

At present, the palace serves the Presidium of the Council of Ministers of the Polish People's Republic, for representative purposes.

In 1965, a reproduction of the equestrian statue of Prince Joseph Poniatowski by the great Danish sculptor Bertel Thorvaldsen, the original of which was destroyed by the Nazis during the last war, was set up in the court-of-honour of the palace.

Many amusing tales and anecdotes are connected with the residence and its former owners, particularly with Prince Karol Radziwiłł, known as 'Panie Kochanku' (which could be translated as Mi' dear) after the Prince's favourite manner of addressing all and sundry, who used the residence during the latter part of the 18th century. Karol Radziwiłł, Palatine of Vilna, scion of a great family, endowed with a great fortune, was a man of little education, a die-hard conservative. He enjoyed tremendous popularity among the petty gentry whom he won over by his extravagance, free and easy familiarity and the eccentricity of his style of life. One of his eccentricities is described by Kazimierz Władysław Wójcicki, a student of Warsaw's history: "My father showed me the spot in the outer court of the Royal Castle, where Prince Karol left his coach harnessed to four great bears, creating a frantic panic among the equipages of the fine lords and ladies, the steeds of high mettle neighing, rearing and breaking loose, creating a tremendous uproar and commotion. The king sent a page to enquire what was the trouble. The page reported that Prince Radziwiłł had arrived to pay his respects to His Majesty, in a carriage drawn by four bears. Radziwiłł had hit on the idea of harnessing his carriage to bears for the good reason that he was called the 'Lithuanian bear' at the court of Stanislaus Augustus."

Prince Karol nurtured a marked distaste for Stanislaus Augustus, which he hardly bothered to conceal, repeatedly reminding the king of his parvenue origins. Wójcicki recounts that one day the prince came to pay his respects to the king wearing a coat very much the worse for wear. "'My good Prince,' the king addressed him kindly, 'you might have a new coat made, don't you think?' 'Your Majesty, Mi' dear,' Radziwiłł replied, 'this coat has been worn by eight Palatines of Vilna before me; no wonder it's a bit off colour.' The answer carried a thinly veiled jibe at the recent date of the rise in rank of the king's family."

View shown on the border of the plan of Warsaw drawn by Pierre Ricaud de Tirregaille, 1762

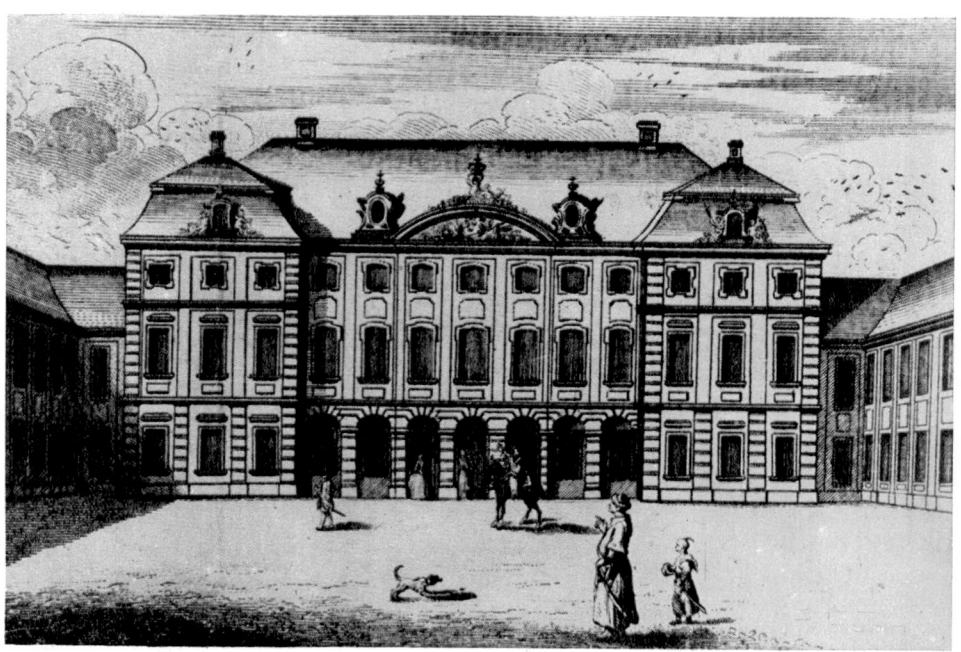

General view with the statue of Prince Joseph Poniatowski in the foreground

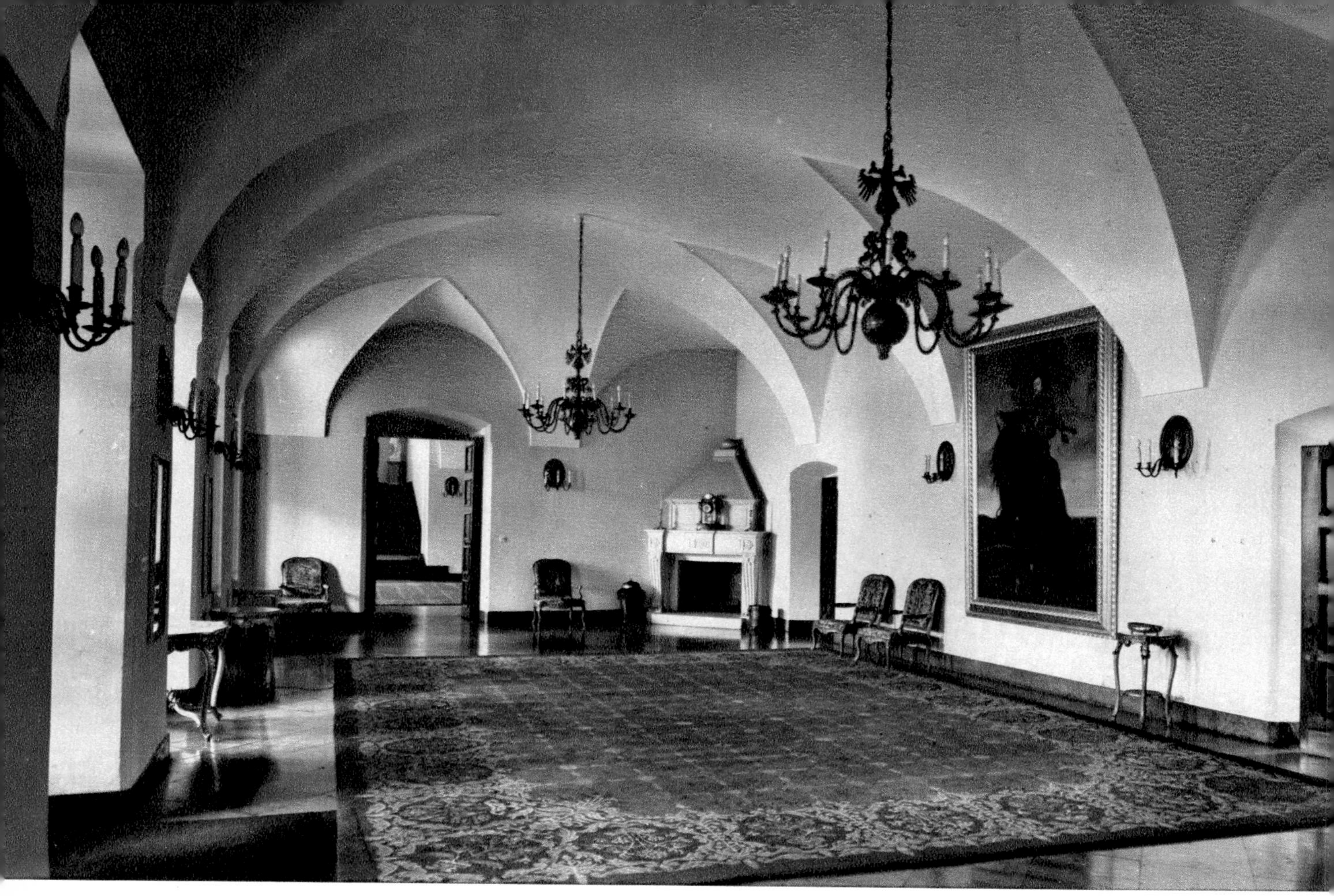

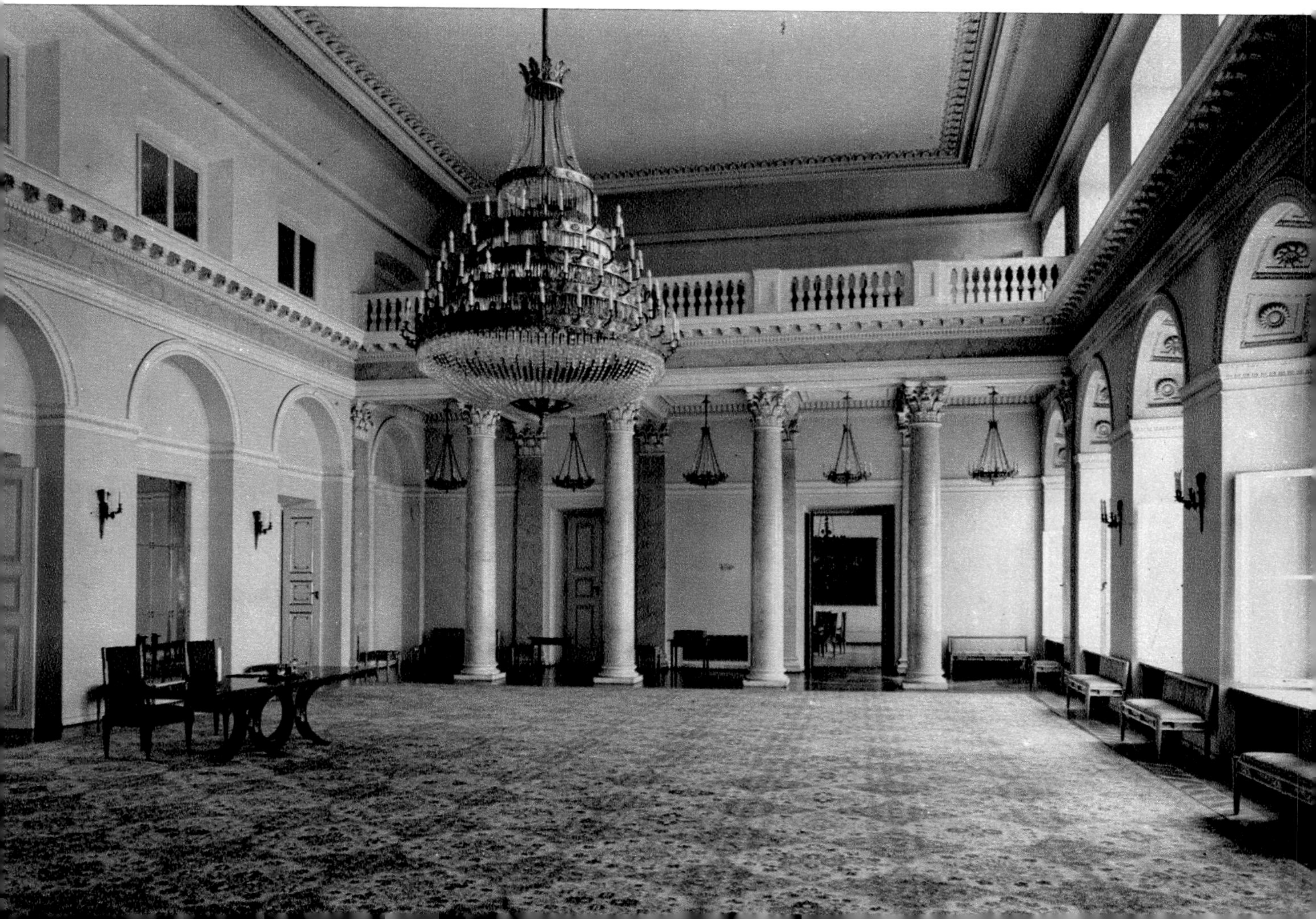

Ground floor vestibule

The Balroom on the first floor

The Diningroom

A bird's eye view of the Palace of the Council of Ministers *(bottom)* and the Potocki Palace *(above)*

The Rau Residence

The possession at the corner of Ujazdowskie Avenue and Piękna Street, together with the building which stood there, was purchased in 1865 by the industrialist Wilhelm Ellis Rau, later one of the founders of the Lilpop, Rau and Loewenstein Metal Concern. Rau engaged the architect Leandro Marconi to convert the existing building into a residence in the style of Italian renaissance. The work was completed in 1868. The building boasted excellent symmetrical proportions, with projections at either end of the front façade, embellished by semi-circular porticos. The reception rooms were situated on the ground floor whereas the living quarters were on the first floor. The kitchens were located in the basement, and a huge English kitchen-stove was brought over especially from Vienna. The residence, though small, represented the last word in contemporary comfort and luxury. It had central heating, gas lighting, and was connected with the sewage system. Well known artists were engaged to decorate the residence. Leandro Marconi sculpted two allegorical statues representing Architecture and Sculpture and Andrzej Pruszyński two others, personifying Painting and Mechanics. These figures were set up at the corners of the front projections. The same artists sculpted eight antique busts adorning the façade of the residence. Another artist, Ludwik Kucharzewski, executed sculptures for the ornamental fountain in the garden and two groups of figures. The painter Jan Strzałecki was commissioned with the interior decorations.

In 1906, the residence was acquired by Maria Branicka née Sapieha, and on her death in 1919, it passed to her daughter, also Maria, married to Jerzy Radziwiłł. The residence was enlarged about the year 1906 by the addition of two short wings on the garden side; a passage was run from the northern side to the adjoining residence, which had once belonged to the Lilpop family, but was then owned by Maria and Jerzy Radziwiłł (this is where the American Embassy now stands). In the 1930s the Radziwiłłs rented the building to the Foreign Ministry as residence of Vice-Minister Jan Szembek. The residence was destroyed during the Warsaw Uprising in 1944. It was rebuilt after the war to serve as the Swiss Embassy, according to plans by the Swiss architect Hans Schmidt. The garden elevation was spoilt by the addition of garages between the two short wings mentioned above. The sculptured figures were not restored. The Ujazdowskie Avenue façade of the residence is undoubtedly the best preserved part of the former Rau residence.

View from Ujazdowskie Avenue before 1939

Present-day view from Ujazdowskie Avenue

View from Piękna Street

Medallion on the Piękna Street elevation

The Sapieha Residence

UL. ZAKROCZYMSKA 6

A Sebastian Rybczyński built himself a manor-house here in the first quarter of the 18th century. Jan Fryderyk Sapieha of Kodeń, Castellan of Troki, acquired the property in 1725. He had the manor-house pulled down and in its place an imposing residence built, according to plans by Jan Zygmunt Deybel. The first stage of the work was carried out between 1731 and 1734, when a residence in late baroque style was built, consisting of the main building and two wings forming a short court-of-honour. In the second stage, carried out between 1736 and 1746, the neighbouring property was acquired and the residence substantially enlarged at the northern and southern ends by the addition of new wings. In 1817, the government of the Kingdom of Poland purchased the residence from the Sapiehas, and between 1818 and 1820 had it converted to military barracks according to designs by Wilhelm Henryk Minter. This conversion completely spoilt the general style of the palace and eliminated all baroque ornaments. The 4th Infantry Regiment, which was to win immortal fame during the November Insurrection, was stationed in those barracks, which came to be known as the Sapieha Barracks (A memorial plaque in honour of the Regiment has been walled into the façade of the building). The 4th Infantry Regiment figures in a great many anecdotes. Recruited mainly from among Varsovians, the Regiment was famous for the perfection of its drill, which made it a favourite of the Grand Duke Constantine, brother of the Tsar Aleksander I, Commander in Chief of the Army of the Kingdom of Poland. "On the other hand", Ignacy Komorowski wrote in his *Memoirs of a Cadet Officer*, "it represented an assortment of rogues and rascals, frauds, humbugs and swindlers, even thieves. But all this was done with an inimitable sort of street-urchinlike humour and gaiety." Komorowski also recounts an amusing episode which happened when the Grand Duke was visiting the 4th Infantry barracks: "One winter day, as the Grand Duke left his carriage at the entrance to the 4th Infantry barracks, he threw his beaver-lined cloak to one of the men on duty outside. As he left the barracks he called for his cloak, but neither the cloak nor the man could be found. There was absolute consternation in the barracks, the strictest of searches continued non-stop for several days, all men being consigned to barracks. But all to no avail and no cloak was found. The Grand Duke laughed at the courage of the rascal who had not hesitated to steal his cloak, and promised that not only would he go unpunished, but would receive a generous recompense, if only he would step forward and own up. Apparently the Grand Duke's promises did not carry much weight because the culprit was never found."

After suppression of the November Insurrection, Russian regiments were stationed in the barracks. During the interwar period the residence also served as a barracks. The building was destroyed in enemy action during the Warsaw Uprising in 1944. It was rebuilt after the war according to plans by Maria Zachwatowicz and has served as a primary school ever since.

Front view of the main building

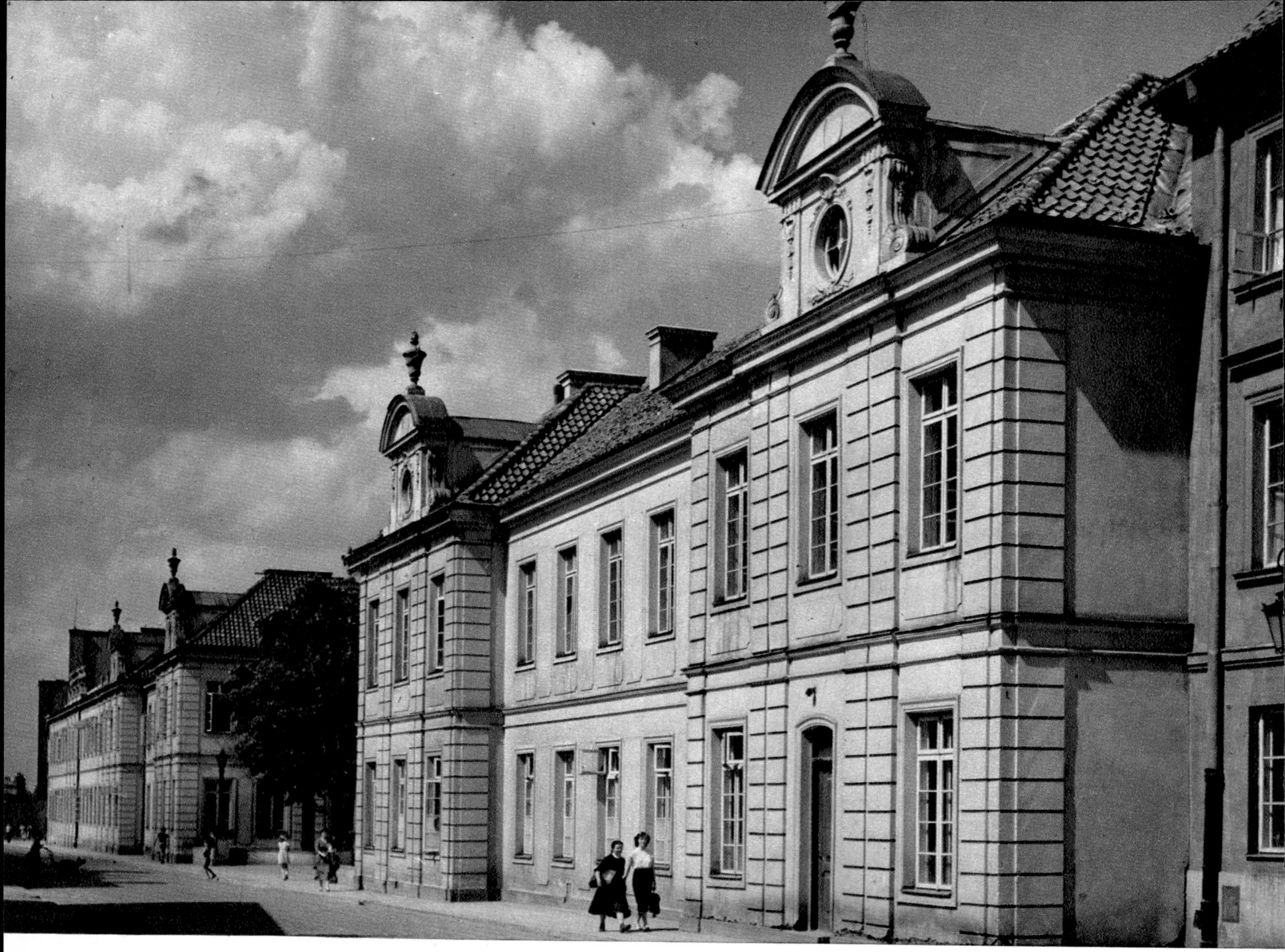

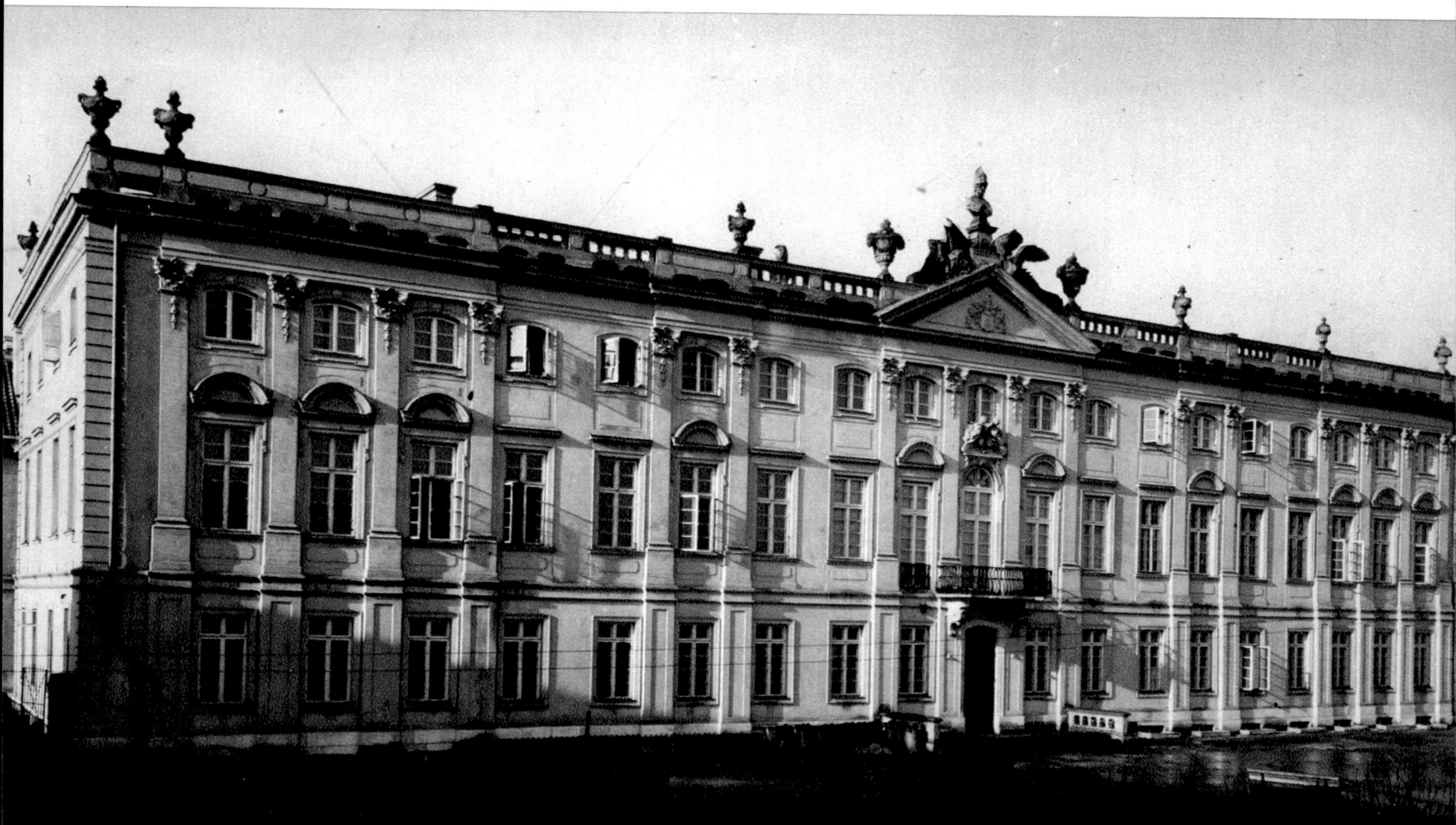

The Sobański Residence
AL. UJAZDOWSKIE 13

The history of this residence has not been entirely clarified as yet. Some Warsaw historians affirm that it was built in Tuscan style between 1852 and 1854, according to plans by Julian Ankiewicz, for Aniela Bławacka, née Ostrowska. Since then it changed hands several times until it was sold to Emilia Sobańska, née Łubieńska, married to Count Feliks Sobański, owner of great estates in the Ukraine, a well-known philanthropist. Other historians contend that the residence was built by the Sobańskis according to designs by Leandro Marconi. At present it is hard to establish whether the Ankiewicz residence was pulled down or just completely rebuilt according to Marconi's plans. The existing residence seems very much a homogeneous structure and nothing indicates that it should have "swallowed up" another earlier building.

The Sobański residence stands some way back from the street flanked on either side by detached picturesque pavilions. The architecture of the residence, painstakingly finished in every detail, carries characteristics of the Italian renaissance. The residence is rightly considered one the most beautiful buildings in Ujazdowskie Avenue. The large gardens at the back were divided up during the period between the wars and at present Przyjaciół Avenue runs where they used to be.

Heavily damaged during the Warsaw Uprising, the Sobański residence was carefully restored after the war. In 1947, it was turned to the Warsaw Conservatoire. At present it is occupied by the Patriotic Movement of National Revival. The bronze figure of David in front of the residence is a copy of the famous sculpture by Donatello.

View of the wing from Zakroczymska Street *(overleaf)*

Garden view of the main building *(overleaf)*

View from Ujazdowskie Avenue before 1939

Present-day view from Ujazdowskie
Avenue

Front elevation with cartouches

Putti on the terrace of the front elevation

The Staszic Palace UL. NOWY ŚWIAT 72

This building was never intended for residential purposes. It was destined for the Royal Society of Friends of Science, but has always been called the Staszic Palace, after the man who conceived the idea of building it and contributed part of the necessary funds. The palace was built according to designs by Antonio Corazzi between 1820 and 1823 on the site of a late baroque Dominican church. The neo-classical façade is surmounted by a small dome, which adds a very appropriate finishing touch to the view down Krakowskie Przedmieście. In his *Historical and Statistical Description of the City of Warsaw*, Łukasz Gołębiowski gave the following description of the Assembly Hall of the Society: "The public assembly hall is adorned by a life-size painting of His Imperial Majesty the King Emperor Alexander I, the work of Professor Blank; a painting of the King of Saxony by Bacciarelli adorns the opposite wall; the sculptures in bas-relief on the walls are the work of Maliński, stuccos and other ornaments are by Vincenti; busts of Albertrandi, Potocki, Naruszewicz, Krasicki, Jan Kochanowski, and Sarbiewski adorn the walls. A large amphitheatre, capable of seating several hundred people, and loges with ornamental Corinthian columns face the space reserved for members of the Society." This hall has not been preserved.

In 1830, the statue of Nicolaus Copernicus, by the great Danish sculptor Bertel Thorvaldsen, was set up in front of the Staszic Palace. The Society occupied the building up till 1832, when it was dissolved by the Tsar Nicolas I. The building was then occupied by offices of the State Lottery; form 1862 it housed a secondary school for boys. In 1893 the building was converted according to plans by a Russian architect Pokrovsky, approved by the Tsar Aleksander III personally. The central part was turned into an Orthodox church, in commemoration of the Shuysky Tsars, who had been buried in a chapel which had once stood on the site. This reconstruction gave the palace an over-decorated façade lined in colourful small bricks in different colours, in imitation of Byzantine and Russian styles. In independent Poland the palace was restored between 1924 and 1926 to its original neo-classical style. Marian Lalewicz, the architect in charge of the work, did not restore the palace exactly to the appearance designed by Antonio Corazzi, for example he did away with the side projections and altered the shape of the dome. During the twenty interwar years, the palace was occupied by the Warsaw Scientific Society. Heavily damaged in the Warsaw Uprising, it was restored between 1946 and 1950 to its appearance in the 1820s by Piotr Biegański who also designed the new wings enclosing the inner courtyard. The building was handed over to the Warsaw Scientific Society and at present it is the seat of the Polish Academy of Sciences.

General view

The Copernicus Monument in front of the building

The Symonowicz Residence

UL. SOLEC 37, UL. IDŹKOWSKIEGO 5

The exact date when this residence was built remains unknown, but it was certainly in existence in 1762, since it figures on Pierre Ricaud de Tirregaille's plan of Warsaw. The official Warsaw property register for 1770 specifies that the owner of the residence was a 'Baron' Simon de Symonowicz, of Armenian origin, owner of landed property in Sandomierz region, nobilitated by Parliament in 1768. The name of the architect who designed it, like the date of its construction, is unknown. The residence was in late baroque style, but its general appearance must have seemed rather traditional in the latter half of the 18th century: its side projections jutted out well to the front, each with its own roof, the whole reminiscent of renaissance manor-houses. Józef Niedziałkowski purchased the property from Symonowicz, only to put it up for sale again in 1788. At the time, buildings appertaining to the residence included annexes, a granary, stables, a coach-house and a large brewery. The property changed hands repeatedly; its rapid decline began in the 19th century. In September 1944, toward the end of the Warsaw Uprising, the residence was in the middle of heavy fighting waged by the Home Army detachment commanded by Lt. Col. Radosław against overwhelming odds. Radosław's unit was supported by a section of the People's Army Assault Battalion, named after the 4th Infantry Regiment. During the night of 15 September, men of the 9th Infantry Regiment of the First Polish Army started crossing the Vistula going to the assistance of the insurgents. The Czerniaków bridgehead was established on 16 September, and there men of the Home Army, the 9th Infantry Regiment and the People's Army fought shoulder to shoulder against hopeless odds until September 22, when the bridgehead was overrun by the enemy. During the fighting, the residence served as a field hospital. Though heavily damaged, it survived the war. Carefully restored in 1951, it was used as the local district library. At present, the residence serves as a preparatory school. A plaque commemorating the landing of First Polish Army soldiers has been set up on the Vistula bank close to the residence.

Many anecdotes are associated with the Symonowicz residence. One of them says this was where Prince Joseph Poniatowski used to meet his pretty Annie. According to another story, towards the end of the 19th century, it was a "house of ill fame".

149

Front elevation

Central projection of the front elevation with a cartouche

The Szlenkier Residence

This residence was built between 1881 and 1883 for a rich industrialist Karol Jan Szlenkier, according to plans by Witold Lanci. Built in line with the street, the residence has an inner courtyard enclosed by wings. The façade of the building was in high Roman renaissance style, while the portal with its two mighty Atlantes supporting the first floor balcony (non-existent now), was modelled on the portal of the Palazzo Davia-Bargellini in Bologna. The steep roof, partly shielded by a balustered parapet, reminiscent of the type of roofs built in France in the late renaissance period, disagreed with the Italian renaissance style of the façade. The ground floor of the residence was occupied by Szlenkier's offices, the first floor by his private apartments and the remaining accommodation served as the quarters of officials and servants. The interiors were kept in renaissance style and among them the most remarkable aspect was presented by the imposing staircase adorned by marble columns with red shafts and white bases and capitals. The wall-paintings were by Wojciech Gerson executed in encaustic technique. The cost of the residence exceeded 300,000 rubles, a very considerable sum of money in those days. The Szlenkier residence was one of the grandest residences of the Warsaw plutocracy at the end of the 19th century.

In 1922, Karol Jan Szlenkier's children sold the residence to the Italian Legation, subsequently raised to the rank of Embassy. A series of alterations were carried out, which partly spoilt the building's style and character. The front part of the building sustained heavy damage during the Warsaw Uprising. The Italian Embassy took possession of the building in 1945, immediately after the war. Its restoration began in 1946, the work being finished the following year. The building underwent thorough repairs and renovation in 1964–65, when it was given its present form. The façade was made considerably simpler by elimination of some of the ornaments, for example, the Atlantes. The elevations on the courtyard side, on the other hand, remain unchanged, and so does the main staircase. The large drawingroom and diningroom on the first floor were given neo-classical stucco ornaments by artists brought over from Italy.

Balcony and first floor windows

Design of the elevation of the Szlenkier Residence by W. Lanci, 1880

Present-day front elevation

The Śleszyński Residence

In the middle of 1826, Stanisław Śleszyński, captain of the engineers, and a gentleman named Józef Fox, set about building a residence in neo-classical style, according to plans by Antonio Corazzi. It was a smallish two-storey building with a deep portico surmounted by a pediment. A two-storey annex was added on the side of the residence where Piękna Street now runs. At the same time, the Śleszyńskis arranged a pleasure garden known as the Swiss Valley on an adjoining piece of hilly terrain. During the first few days following the outbreak of the November Insurrection, the Artillery Staff established its headquarters in the residence; it is said that the Chief of Staff, General Ignacy Prądzyński, planned his military operations here.

After the collapse of the Insurrection, the Śleszyńskis began letting their residence, in 1843, for example, to British Consul, Gustavus Charles du Plat. The property remained in the Śleszyński family up to 1852, after which it changed hands repeatedly. Between 1863 and 1912 it belonged to the Lessers, a well-known banking family, from whom it was purchased by Ryszard Edward Kimens, who sold it the next year to Franciszek Salezy Potocki of Peczara. At the time, the residence housed a Russian art club, and a dairy stood in its gardens. In 1928, two thirds of the property passed to the Strzemieszyce Industrial Concern and one third (the residence itself) to Janusz Kirchmajer. The residence and annex were in very poor condition throughout the period between the wars. Rumours spread that the place was haunted and nobody could live there because of inexplicable happenings which took place at night. The residence and annex were destroyed during the Second World War. It was rebuilt by Helena and Szymon Syrkus between 1947 and 1948, destined to serve as the Yugoslav embassy.

Front elevation before 1939

Present-day elevation

Detail of the portico

The Tyszkiewicz Residence

This building was founded by Ludwik Tyszkiewicz, Field Hetman of the Grand Duchy of Lithuania, who married Konstancja Poniatowska, niece of Stanislaus Augustus. The king must have a great liking for the Tyszkiewicz family, since he married off his other niece Teresa also to a scion of the family, Wincenty Tyszkiewicz, Grand Referendary of Lithuania.

In 1781, Ludwik Tyszkiewicz commissioned Stanisław Zawadzki to build him a residence. In 1786 when the walls had reached first floor level, for some reason, the Field Hetman cancelled the contract with Zawadzki and commissioned the court architect Jan Chrystian Kamsetzer to finish the work. Kamsetzer undertook to make plans and drawings both of the exterior and interiors, supervise the work personally, and deal with the question of interior decorations. Building and decorating work continued up to 1792. To help with the interior decorations Kamsetzer employed stucco workers Paolo Casasopra, Giuseppe Amadio and Jan Michał Graff, who worked for him regularly, as well as Józef Probst and Giuseppe Borghi, the sculptor Johann Duldt and the painter Wawrzyniec Jasiński. The two Atlantes supporting the balcony on the Krakowskie Przedmieście side were the work of the court sculptor André le Brun and his assistant Giacomo Contieri.

The Tyszkiewicz residence stands in line with other buildings in Krakowskie Przedmieście. Kamsetzer took pains only over the Krakowskie Przedmieście elevation and the one facing the square in front of the Church of the Visitation Sisters, but spared little or no interest for the rear elevations in the courtyard. As regards the interior, the entrance hall and staircase with four columns supporting the landing, reminiscent of the vestibule and staircase of the Blank residence in Senatorska Street, were particularly notable. The main reception rooms on the first floor faced Krakowskie Przedmieście. Most resplendent among them were the great, two storeys high, diningroom kept in a white colour scheme, the grand drawingroom, also two storeys high, with conch ceilinged apses at either end, and also the billiards-room with stucco ornaments on the walls.

When Ludwik Tyszkiewicz died in 1808 the residence passed to his daughter Anna, wife of Aleksander Potocki, and later of Stanisław Dunin-Wąsowicz. She was famed for her wit and humour; her memoirs *Reminiscences of an Eye-Witness,* were recently reissued. In 1840, August Potocki, her elder son by the first marriage, bought the residence from his mother; after his death it passed to his younger brother Maurycy, and in 1879 to the latter's son, August, popularly known as Count Gucio, undoubtedly one of Warsaw's most colourful figures at the close of the 19th century. A gay buck, famed for his revelries, hero of countless anecdotes, Count Gucio won the heart of the people of Warsaw by the aloof disdain which he showed the detested Russian Governor-General Josif Hurka. Stefan Krzywoszewski, a comedy writer and author of very interesting memoirs, gave the following description of Count Gucio: "Friendly and easy-going, with a ready smile, fond of spicy stories and piquant jokes, with the lavish generosity of a grand seigneur, his popularity was further increased by the way he kept ostentatiously aloof from the Castle, steadfastly refusing all honours and dignities. Count Gucio was fond of beautiful ladies of none too strict virtue, noble wines, good shooting and high stakes at gambling. He kept company with the gay and witty, paying no attention to their origins or social position. He was perfectly incapable of managing his great fortune, which included the estates of Jabłonna and Nieporęt near Warsaw, the beautiful residence in Krakowskie Przedmieście, the castle and estate of Zator in Galicia and the great forest estate of Berezyna. These properties should have been bringing him a very substantial revenue, instead of which Count Gucio was constantly in financial straits. The bailiff was a by no means uncommon sight at his Krakowskie Przedmieście residence. Count Gucio would receive him with amused unconcern and occasionally offer him a cup of choice champagne.

"In society circles, he was viewed with severity, and disapproval was expressed at his prodigal whims and loose dissolute way of life. But during Race Week when his great open carriage harnessed to four magnificent thoroughbreds appeared in Ujazdowskie Avenue, all eyes would follow the splendid equipage and smile knowingly: 'There goes Count Gucio!' "

The residence itself remained virtually unchanged throughout the 19th century, but another annex was added to the side facing the Church of the Visitation Sisters, also a gate leading to the rear courtyard, designed by Fryderyk Albert Lessel. New stables, a coach-house and an orangery were built round the courtyard between 1841 and 1846, according to plans by Henryk Marconi who also redecorated the residence interiors, introducing some alterations. Some of the rooms were decorated in neo-renaissance style. Two Italian artists were engaged for the painting decorations, Michele Chiarini and Leati, whose first name has been forgotten.

When Count Gucio died in 1905, his fortune, together with the residence, passed to his only son Maurycy. In 1923, Maurycy Potocki sold the residence to the National Savings Bank. During the period between the wars it was used by the Polish Academy of Literature and housed a collection of historical documents belonging to the National Library. During the Warsaw Uprising, the residence was burnt down by enemy action. Rebuilt between 1948 and 1956 by Jan Dąbrowski, it was handed over to Warsaw University. The entrance hall and staircase, diningroom, grand drawingroom and billiards-room were restored almost exactly to their original state, but as regards other rooms, this unfortunately proved impossible. At present, the residence houses the Section of Drawings and Engravings of the Warsaw University Library and other collections.

View of the Tyszkiewicz Residence from the north, by Zygmunt Vogel, c. 1792

Front elevation

Atlantes supporting the first floor balcony

Northern elevation

The Shell Room on the first floor

Detail of decoration

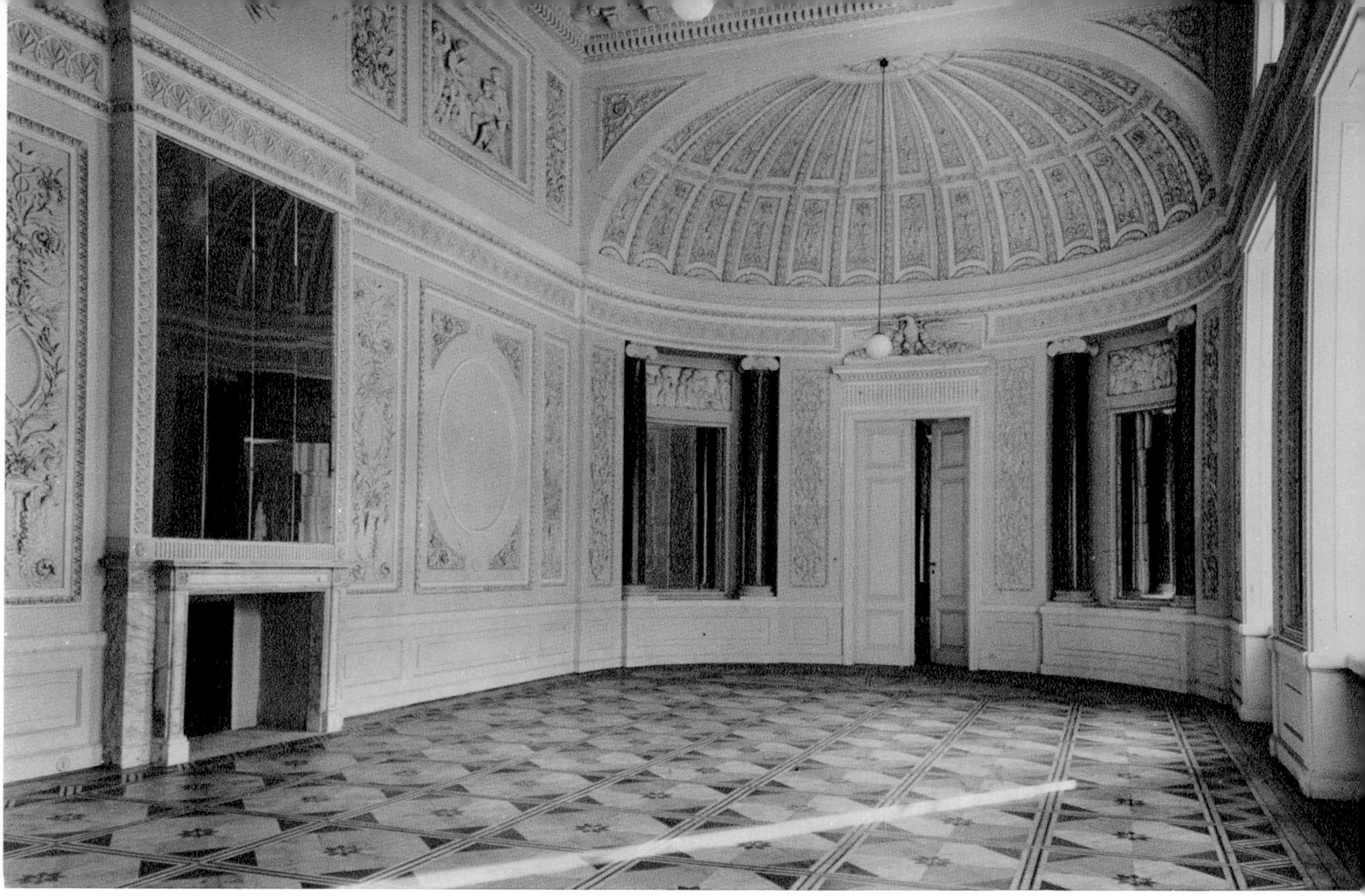

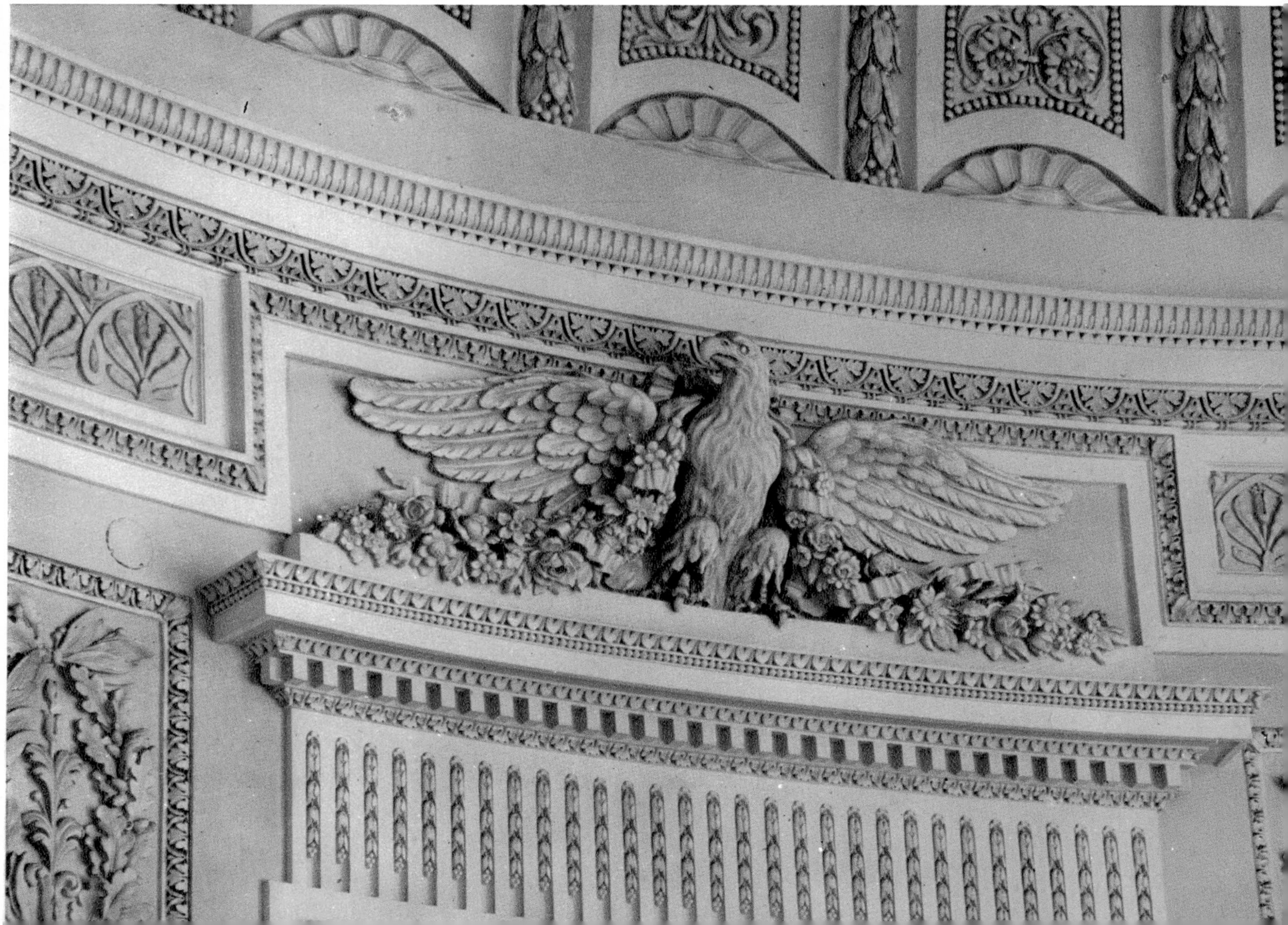

The Uruski Residence (also known as the Czetwertyński Residence) UL. KRAKOWSKIE PRZEDMIEŚCIE 30

On the site where the Uruski residence now stands a late baroque mansion was built at the end of the 1730s for Stanisław Poniatowski, Castellan of Cracow, father of Stanislaus Augustus, according to plans attributed to Jan Zygmunt Deybel. In 1762, the residence passed to Kazimierz Poniatowski, Lord High Chamberlain of the Crown, brother to the king. It was in this residence that Stanislaus Augustus first heard the news that he had been elected king. The residence figures on the painting by Bernardo Bellotto called Canaletto which shows Krakowskie Przedmieście from Nowy Świat Street. The property changed hands repeatedly until in 1843 it was acquired by Seweryn Uruski, leader of the gentry of Warsaw Province, privy councillor and Steward at the Russian Imperial Court, well-known expert on heraldry. Uruski had the Poniatowski residence pulled down and in its place built a new one according to plans by Andrzej Gołoński, who gave the new building certain characteristics of the renaissance style. Work began in 1844 and was not completed till 1847. The two-storey building has two side projections, each a storey higher than the main body and divided by Corinthian pilasters. The centre piece of the front elevation is surmounted by a large cartouche with the armorial bearings of the Uruskis sculpted by Ludwik Kaufman. Before the last war, a porte cochère used to lead through the end projection on the left-hand side of the residence to the courtyard enclosed by annexes. The front elevation is symmetrical; in contrast to it, the façade which faces the street leading to the Kazimierzowski Palace, is picturesquely asymmetrical and boasts a turret. The owner and his family occupied only the main body of the residence, the annexes contained apartments to let. When Seweryn Uruski died in 1890, the residence passed to his widow Ermancja née Tyzenhauz, and after her death, to their daughter Maria, who in 1872 married Prince Włodzimierz Światopełk-Czetwertyński. The residence was restored between 1893 and 1895 under the supervision of Józef Huss, who built a new northern annex facing toward the East, in place of the old one, in semi-ruined state, which probably dated back to the days of Stanislaus Poniatowski. The ground floor of the new annex served as a coach-house. The floors above were occupied by apartments to let. Huss also altered the general aspect of the remaining annexes. The residence remained in the Czetwertyński family till 1946, when it became the property of Warsaw University. It was destroyed during the war, set on fire by the Nazis and burnt down to the ground after the collapse of the Warsaw Uprising. Rebuilt between 1948 and 1951 by Jan Dąbrowski, it now houses the Geographical Institute of Warsaw University.

Front elevation

The Wessel Residence

UL. KRAKOWSKIE PRZEDMIEŚCIE 25

This residence was also called the Ostrowski residence, and sometimes the Old Post-Office. It was built about the middle of the 18th century, since in 1762 Pierre Ricaud de Tirregaille drew it on the border of his plan of Warsaw. Some time after 1750, this late baroque residence belonged to Franciszek Jan Załuski, Starost of Grójec, who sold it in 1761 to Teodor Wessel, Treasurer of the Crown. In turn, Wessel sold it in 1764 to Antoni Ostrowski, Bishop of Kujawy, subsequently Primate of Poland. The residence kept changing hands. In 1780 it was bought by Franciszek Ignacy Przebendowski, Palatine of Pomerania, Director General of the Post, to serve as the central post-office. In the register of properties recorded after the death of Stanislaus Augustus, the residence figures as the king's private property, and as such passed to his heir, Prince Joseph Poniatowski. A certain Schultz figures as the next owner of the residence. In 1805, Schultz sold the property to the General Postamt in Berlin. The post-office remained in the building up to 1874. When Trębacka Street was enlarged in 1882, a corner house adjoining the residence was pulled down. The residence itself was put up for sale, with the stipulation that the purchaser would cede "two ells" of the building to permit further enlargement of Trębacka Street. In effect, the residence underwent basic reconstruction according to plans by Aleksander Woyde and Władysław Marconi; a corner of the building was cut away and the residence acquired a new elevation facing enlarged Trębacka Street. At the same time, a third floor was added to the building in order to increase its rental. The new façade and additional floor harmonized perfectly with the existing architecture of the building. From 1887, for a time, the residence housed the offices of the daily *Kurier Codzienny* and the weekly *Tygodnik Ilustrowany*. During the period between the wars, the building housed a well-known antique-shop. It was burnt down during the Warsaw Uprising in 1944. Rebuilt after the war according to plans by Jan Bieńkowski, it was restored to its appearance in 1882. At present it is occupied by the Office of the Procurator General.

View shown on the border of the plan of Warsaw drawn by
Pierre Ricaud de Tirregaille, 1762

Front elevation

The Eliza Wielopolska Residence AL. UJAZDOWSKIE 15

This residence was built between 1875 and 1876 for Antoni Nagórny, head of the Department of Trade and Industry in the Bank of Poland, according to plans by Józef Huss. When in 1877 a new street, known as Aleja Róż (Avenue of Roses) was laid out at right angles to Ujazdowskie Avenue, the property on which the residence stood became a corner site. The little residence consisted of a square shaped main body facing Ujazdowskie Avenue, with an extended annex at the back. Its elevations reverted to the traditions of the Italian renaissance and the late neo-classical style, characteristic of the Berlin architecture of the period. Originally, the disposition of rooms on the ground and first floor of the residence was almost identical, but later, major changes were introduced in the lay-out of the interiors.

The residence changed hands repeatedly; between 1898 and 1932 it was owned by the Marchioness Eliza Wielopolska, who undertook its thorough reconstruction in 1904. The *Kurier Warszawski* of 27 November 1904 wrote that "the interiors of the residence of the Marchioness Eliza Wielopolska, at the corner of Ujazdowskie Avenue and Avenue of Roses, are undergoing complete conversion, electric lighting is being installed, etc. Work is continuing in the whole building, and is not expected to be completed before the middle of next month. The Marchioness, who arrived in Warsaw yesterday, had to put up at the Europejski Hotel."

The residence, undamaged in the last war, now serves as the British Embassy.

Front elevation before 1939

168

Present-day view
Balcony and first floor window

The Wierzbicki Residence
UL. GROCHOWSKA 64/66

Various legends are attached to this residence which is said to have been built toward the end of the 18th century by Primate Michał Poniatowski. During the battle of Grochów, at the beginning of the November Insurrection in 1830, General Józef Chłopicki is said to have established his headquarters there; Stanisław Wyspiański set the action of his play *Warszawianka* (The Varsovienne) within its walls. Cannonballs embedded in the walls of the residence seem to substantiate these legends. Recent research, however, has established that the residence was built in the 1830s, for Charles Osterloff, a Swede who purchased part of the Grochów estate and built there a brewery, a spirits distillery and a wine-cellar where champagne-type wine was matured. The residence is a modest building in neo-renaissance style with a hipped tiled roof, standing in a large park. In 1924, it was acquired by Andrzej Wierzbicki, a prominent politician and economist, who carried out fundamental restoration of the building between 1925 and 1927, according to plans by Zdzisław Kalinowski and Maksymilian Goldberg. During the Second World War, the residence was badly damaged and looted. Restored in 1956, it now houses a school of music.

Front view

The Zamoyski Residence

UL. FOKSAL 2/4

This residence was built in 1878 in the style of the late French renaissance, for Konstanty Zamoyski, according to plans by Leandro Marconi. It consists of the main building and two detached wings standing at right angles to it and forming a broad front courtyard ending on Foksal Street. It was built in the middle of extensive gardens laid out in the mid-18th century, which formerly extended right up to Nowy Świat Street; at a later date the gardens were named Vauxhall for some unknown reason, which was gradually polonised to Foksal. When Konstanty Zamoyski acquired the property in 1870, the end extremities of the gardens were divided up and sold, on condition that villas would be built on the sites, whereas the central part of the gardens was reserved for a new street, which was to run up to Nowy Świat, but the street was not laid out till 1880. Though heavy fighting was waged in this area during the Warsaw Uprising, the residence escaped damage. At present, it houses the Association of Polish Architects. Between 1964 and 1968, the Association had an exhibition pavilion built, attached to the northern end of the main building, which does not spoil the general appearance of the residence. The popular Foksal Gallery which occupies the ground floor of the left wing, provides platform for avant-garde art.

Front view

Garden view

Gate leading to the courtyard

Select Bibliography

Readers desirous of more detailed information on Warsaw's palaces and residences should acquaint themselves with the series entitled Zabytki Warszawy (Warsaw's Historic Buildings), published by the State Scientific Publishers (PWN), and in particular with the following books:

Bania, Z., and Jaroszewski, T. S.: *Pałac Rady Ministrów* (to appear); Bartczakowa, A.: *Pałac Paca* (1973); Bartczakowa, A., and Malinowska, I: *Pałac Branickich* (1974); Jaroszewski, T. S.: *Pałac Kossakowskich* (1977); Jaroszewski, T. S.: *Pałac Lubomirskich* (1971); Jaroszewski, T. S.: *Pałac Szlenkierów* (1975); Król, A., and Król-Kaczorowska, B.: *Pałac Pod Blachą* (1974); Kwiatkowska, M.: *Pałac Raczyńskich* (1980); Kwiatkowska, M. I.: *Pałac Tyszkiewiczów* (1973); Kwiatkowska, M. I.: *Pałac Uruskich* (1974); Kwiatkowska, M. I., and Malinowska, I.: *Pałac Potockich* (1976); Kwiatkowski, M.: *Belweder* (1976); Kwiatkowski, M.: *Pałac Blanka* (1974); Kwiatkowski, M.: *Królikarnia* (1971); Kwiatkowski, M.: *Pałac Morsztynów* (1971); Lorentz, S.: *Natolin* (1970); Malinowska, I.: *Pałac Sapiehów* (1972); Mieleszko, J.: *Pałac Czapskich* (1971); Mossakowski, S.: *Pałac Krasińskich* (1972); Rottermund, A.: *Pałac Błękitny* (1970).

In writing this book, the author made use of the above monographs, as well as books on architects who worked in Warsaw in the 17th, 18th and 19th centuries, for example: Bartczakowa, A.: *Franciszek Maria Lanci 1799–1875* (Warsaw 1954); Bartczakowa, A.: *Jakub Fontana architekt warszawski XVIII wieku* (Warsaw 1970); Batowski, N. and Z., and Kwiatkowski, M.: *Jan Chrystian Kamsetzer architekt Stanisława Augusta* (Warsaw 1978); Jaroszewski, T. S.: *Chrystian Piotr Aigner architekt warszawskiego klasycyzmu* (Warsaw 1970); Jaroszewski, T. S., and Rottermund, A.: *Jakub Hempel, Fryderyk Albert Lessel, Henryk Ittar, Wilhelm Henryk Minter – architekci polskiego klasycyzmu* (Warsaw 1974); Kwiatkowski, M.: *Szymon Bogumił Zug architekt polskiego oświecenia* (Warsaw 1971); Mossakowski, S.: *Tylman z Gameren architekt polskiego baroku* (Wrocław-Warsaw-Cracow-Gdańsk 1973); Tatarkiewicz, W.: *Dominik Merlini* (Warsaw 1954).

The author is also greatly indebted to three M. A. theses prepared at the Seminar on the History of Modern Art at the History of Art Institue, Warsaw University: Grygiel, T.: *Architekt Józef Huss 1846–1904* (Warsaw 1976); Merkel, M.: *Architektura willowa Warszawa drugiej połowy XIX wieku* (Warsaw 1977); Sosnowski, P.: *Pałac w Ursynowie* (Warsaw 1978), all manuscripts in the Library of the History of Art Institute, Warsaw University.

Translated by
Stanisław Tarnowski

Designed by
Jerzy Kępkiewicz

Production editor
Wiesława Zielińska

On the jacket: The Sapieha Residence and the Dziewulski Residence

This is the two thousand and forty-eighth publication of Interpress Publishers

This book appears also in Polish, French and German

Copyright by Polish Interpress Agency 1984

PRINTED IN POLAND

Zakłady Wklęsłodrukowe RSW „Prasa-Książka-Ruch" Warszawa